MYSTERIOUS

EXPLORER:

SOLVING THE PUZZLE OF

AN AFRICAN EXPLORER IN AMERICA—

180 YEARS BEFORE COLUMBUS

NEW EVIDENCE FOR ABU BAKR II IN THE AMERICAN SOUTHWEST—CIRCA 1312 CE

THIS BOOK REVEALS MANY ELEPHANT AND CAMEL

PETROGLYPHS, TRANSLATES AFRICAN WRITINGS,

SOLVES FOUR MYSTERIES IN THE SPANISH RECORDS,

AND EXPLAINS FOUR PIECES OF PUEBLO INDIAN ART

AS WELL AS ONE DINÉ (NAVAJO) MYTH.

Ronald Stewart

BY RONALD STEWART, PH. D

i

ISBN-13: 978-1719051736
ISBN-10: 1719051739

This book was written solely for educational and teaching purposes by a
former educator and professional researcher under the moral rights and
fair use doctrine of Section 107 of the Copyright Act as the author
understands it.

All pictures are from Wikipedia Commons or the internet unless
otherwise noted. The author has done his best to identify, locate, and
request permission from copyright holders. The author respectfully asks
users to contact the author if they have information about the identity or
address of copyright holders whom he was unable to reach. He will be
happy to take the appropriate steps to obtain permission.

*Cover collage of Mali Emperor Abu Bakr II approaching a
New Mexican Pueblo on an African elephant at sunset,
probably as the Pueblo Indians of the Rio Grande Valley
saw him circa 1312 CE, was created by Dr. Ronald Stewart.
Green area at bottom of front cover represents the Rio
Grande Valley's vegetation so important as elephant fodder.*

TABLE OF CONTENTS

ACKNOWLEDGEMENTS

I would like to take this opportunity to extend my heartfelt thanks to the following individuals who contributed knowledge, critically reviewed the draft manuscript or took the time to suggest improvements to my story: Mr. Larry Baker, Executive Director of the San Juan County Archaeological Research Center and Library at Salmon Ruins; Cecilia Bell, New Mexico State Director, Southern Trails Chapter, Oregon-California Trails Association; Dr. John Bell; Mr. Harvey Buchalter, retired teacher, historian, Yiddish translator, and author; Mr. Charles I. Cole, retired Federal employee and life-long friend; Mr. David Freeman, friend; Mr. Andres Grajeda; Ms Elizabeth Horodowich, scholar; Mr. Clay Johnston, Site Steward for Northwest New Mexico; Mr. Xavier Madrid, scholar; Mr. Ethan Ortega, Coronado Historic Site Ranger; Jason Parret, Flora Vista, New Mexico student; Mr. Wilson Poola, Hopi kachina craftsman; Dr. Joseph P. Sánchez, retired Superintendent of Petroglyph National Monument, Editor of Colonial Latin American Historical Review *(CLAHR)* and Director of the Spanish Colonial Research Center, National Park Service; Dr. Brit Allan Storey, United States Bureau of Reclamation senior historian, retired, and Mrs. Patricia Walkow, author, editor, and bon vivant.

A special salute to the Navajo Mythmaker who described the Wo'ia'zhini Dine'è (Black Ant People) thusly: *"came a whole crowd of beings. Dark colored they were, with thick lips and dark, protruding eyes"* — Diné *(Navajo) Nihodilhil (Black World) Creation Myth.*

DEDICATION

This book is hereby dedicated

to the memory of Professor

Donald C. Cutter (1922 – 2014)

Those Who Guessed—or Knew

The Terrestrial Sphere of Crates of Mallus (circa 150 BCE)

****

The earth *"is divided into three parts, one of which is called Asia, the second Europe, the third Africa. . . . Apart from these three parts of the world there exists a fourth part, beyond the ocean, which is unknown to us"*

—*Isadore of Seville, Etymologies (circa 600 CE)*

****

In 1246 CE, a French Geographer stated that *"A man could go around the world, ... as a fly makes the tour of an apple."* From Toby Lester's, *The Fourth Part of the World*

****

"A man traveled so far over land and sea that, circumnavigating the earth, he had come to his own borders." attributed to Sir John Mandeville, but which may have been written by someone else between 1356 - 1366 CE

INTRODUCTION

"It is by doubting that we come to investigate, and by investigating that we recognize the truth."— Peter Abelard

I was perusing some magazines one day a few years ago, when I ran across an article titled "The Maps That Columbus Used" by Jill Withrow Baker. In this article she mentioned "One inscription in Arizona that accompanies a rough drawing of an elephant...." Of course, I was immediately intrigued—and doubtful (as is one of my reviewers to this day). I asked myself: How could this be? How come none of the Southwest literature that I have read even alludes to elephants in the prehistoric North American Southwest? Mammoths yes, Mastodons yes, Gomphotheres yes, *but not Elephants!* Intrigued by this inconsistency, I delved further into the relevant literature. What I found amazed me to no end. There in the Afro-centrist literature (which, by the way, is not taken seriously enough by other American Historians) was the Egyptian Historian Al Umari's description of an African Emperor who set sail to the west with 2000 ships and was never heard of again. Case closed, as far as everyone but Afro-centrists were concerned. This intrigued me even further. How could even the most inept sea captain lose all 2000 of his ships? The answer is—The Mali Emperor did not. Perhaps not all of his ships made it to the unknown world, but his and others did survive. The evidence does exist—if you are willing to open your mind and accept Spanish document mysteries, American Indian myths, pictures, sculptures and shell bead trading as historical records and if you can accept lithic records written in an obscure African language. I couldn't just ignore what I had uncovered. I had to let the world know that the Spanish were <u>not</u> the first non-Americans to visit the North American Southwest—thus this book of History extolling the accomplishments, impact on Native Americans and trail markers of the "Mysterious Explorer".

I still was not totally convinced when I visited the Arizona State Museum on the campus of The University of Arizona in Tucson—not convinced, that is, until I held the Flora Vista, New Mexico, "Elephant Slabs" in my own hands. These were <u>not</u> fakes. These definitely were <u>not</u> somebody's "cowboy doodles" <u>nor</u> "cattle brands" <u>nor</u> "Mormon images". Here were authentic Mandinka inscriptions with a written catalog record pertaining to their discovery and journey from an abandoned Indian pueblo ruin in New Mexico to the Arizona State Museum. The slabs practically shout their authenticity. They are so compelling that they draw you in. I immediately set about deciphering as much of the "elephant slabs" as I could, based on deciphered Sahara Desert stone inscriptions. I was able to read seven signs for "land of inundation" and two symbols for "stone hut" (pueblo) associated with them. Also, there may be symbols for "sunrise", "sunset", "storm", "lightning storm", "lightning" and "residue". A search of the internet revealed images of elephant and camel petroglyphs in the American Southwest, as well as other indicators. Altogether, eighteen indicators have been found in the Southwest as well as three written proofs of exploration by West Africans.

In addition, this history of the Southwest solves many of the mysteries presently existing in Spanish records, Navajo (Diné) myths, petroglyphs, Pueblo Indian kiva paintings and *kachinas*, and of course mysterious Mandinka language inscriptions complete with outlines of elephants, birds and even an unfortunate dog (or some other unlucky quadruped). It explains the origin of Black and dark people mentioned in records of Spanish Capitán Carlos Cantú, Franciscan missionary Francisco Hermenegildo Tomás Garcés, and Spanish settlers in California. And it explains the local Indian name for a spring/watering hole in Baja California. Petroglyphs previously identified as dinosaur, mammoth, rhino, bear, etc. turn out to be Sahara desert camels and African elephants. So-called cowboy doodlings and cattle brands are now recognized as 14th century writings of the so-called "secret society" of elites of the Mali Empire. These are not only meaningful symbols of an African exploration of the North American Southwest, but of even greater significance, are probably the <u>first written descriptions of a prehistoric flood in the Western Hemisphere</u>—inscribed in stone—not in English, Spanish nor in a Native American language, but in a West African language. After all, if you intend to leave a permanent record, you had better leave it <u>inscribed in stone</u>. Besides, what other choice of writing materials did the flood's eye witness have—the fleshy pads of prickly pear cactus?

However, not all seemingly went well with the Mali Emperor's expedition. Some of the sailors or imperial court members possibly died of scurvy on reaching St. Thomas in the Virgin Islands (not unlike the many Plymouth Pilgrims who succumbed to "The General Disease" in 1620).

Members of the expedition had to endure lightning storms during the Southwest's monsoon season. Elephants apparently became sick while traversing the sparse vegetative terrain of Northeastern Arizona. And then the final blow came when the Emperor himself disappeared with not even a monument marking his grave—if indeed he ever had a grave. It is the author's unproven opinion that the "Mysterious Explorer" failed in his quest to circumnavigate the world when his new Pacific Ocean flotilla ran out of potable water or when the stormy Pacific overwhelmed his Pacific fleet. This kind of calamity would indeed mean "Case Closed".

Martin Buber is quoted as saying "All journeys have secret destinations of which the traveler is unaware." Abu Bakr II certainly experienced his "secret destination" with persistence and courage.

Probable route of Abu Bakr II from the Mali Empire to Pacific Ocean

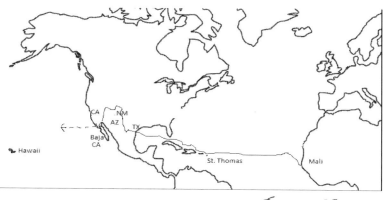

Ronald Stewart

PREFACE

Since there was no report of any member of the Abu Bakr II expedition across the Atlantic Ocean ever returning to the Mali Empire, it appears that few people in Mali, Africa, thought their emperor had survived such a daring exploit— especially not any jeli/griot (oral historian/musician/praise singer). The jeliw/griots were, in fact, ashamed of their emperor because he did not return home with anything beneficial for his family, society or empire.

MALI EMPIRE, WEST AFRICA

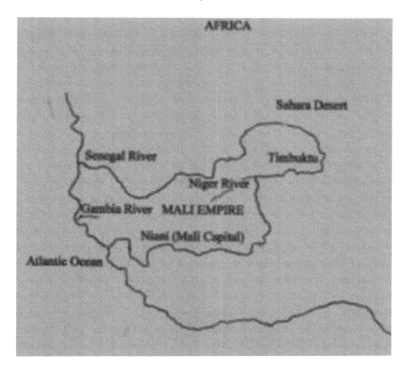

Abu Bakr II's West African Empire circa 1310 CE. Map drawn by Ronald Stewart.

The Mali Empire's King of Kings, Abu Bakr II (aka Abubakari II), ventured into the foggy waters to the west of his empire, which was well documented by Egyptian historian Al Umari in Egypt in 1324 CE. He and his caravan of elephants, camels and probably hundreds of subjects explored the North American Southwest, which has been generally ignored—except by Afro-centrists. Why hasn't this mysterious emperor's fantastic journey been studied by professional historians? Perhaps it's because as a Wikipedia entry for "Abu Bakr II" states:

> Most archaeologists, anthropologists, ethno-historians, linguists, and other modern pre-Columbian scholars say that there is no evidence of any such voyage reaching the Americas, and that there are insufficient evidential grounds to suppose there has been contact between Africa and the New World at any point in the pre-Columbian era. For views representative of this point of view, see the considerations on the question advanced in Haslip-Viera *et al.* (1997), who for example note "no genuine African artifact has ever been found in a controlled archaeological excavation in the New World". See also the supporting responses in peer-review printed in the article, by David Browman, Michael D. Coe, Ann Cyphers, Peter Furst, and other academics active in the field. Ortiz de Montellano *et al.* (1997, *passim.*) continues the case against

Africa-Americas contacts. Other prominent Mesoamerican specialists such as UCR Riverside [University of California] anthropology professor Karl Taube are confident that "There simply is no material evidence of any Pre-Hispanic contact between the Old World and Mesoamerica before the arrival of the Spanish in the sixteenth century".

Contrary to these learned professionals' opinions, this author has found plenty of "evidence" throughout the North American Southwest. No Southwestern historian, until now, has found the indicators that show that this emperor made a journey through the North American Southwest. Indicators and proofs vary from descriptive Spanish records, petroglyphs of elephants and camels, Pueblo Indian wall paintings, *kachinas,* geographical names—and the first written description of a prehistoric flood in the New World, written in stone with elite Mali "Secret Society's" Mande/Mandinka symbols.

Since Archeologists have found no artifacts in context that they have identified as African trade items, they may have been primarily cowrie shells, which could have been misidentified as shells from American shores. Other trade items, like umbrellas, cloth, etc. would have been organic and thus undoubtedly disintegrated over the seven hundred year interim. In addition, most archeological excavations occur within Pueblo ruins, not out in open lowlands where the Emperor's caravan would have set up camps.

The indicators previously have been misidentified. An Indian *kiva* painting was said to be a water priest, spirit or clown. The *kachina* was called *Chakwaina* "the ogre" by at least one pueblo. A state archeologist explained away the stone and pottery elephant inscriptions as pictures of circus elephants which the Indians had seen, while a curator of collections classified them as "cowboy doodlings" or "cattle brands". Barry Fell, an epigrapher, even tried to decipher the stone inscriptions using Micronesian and Indonesian symbols. Best of all, some photographers, and others, believe that the petroglyphs are pictures of mammoths, mastodons and even weirder—of dinosaurs that they supposed were contemporary with humans.

Over-emphasis on Christopher Columbus' (Cristóbal Colón) accomplishments—due in part to the "hype" surrounding the 1893 World's Columbian Exposition in Chicago which celebrated Columbus' so-called "Discovery"—led to the over-looking of other explorers of the New World until proof of a Scandinavian settlement at L'Anse aux Meadows, Newfoundland, Canada, came to light. There are credible indications of many "discoveries".

Saint Brendan and his monks are said to have sailed for a western land. Author: Franciscan Sisters of the Perpetual Adoration (La Crosse, Wis.). Illustration has no restrictions.

Dr. Joseph P. Sánchez has stated that in 1914, Julián Juderías, a Spanish intellectual, "observed that anti-Spanish misconceptions had continued to develop unabated long after their usefulness as propaganda had been served. Juderías argued that anti-Spanish, indeed, anti-Hispanic distortions in both Europe and the Americas constituted a *Leyenda Negra*, or black legend."[1]

Ethnocentric prejudice gives new meaning to the "Black Legend". Although the original "Black Legend" was a Dutch/English diatribe against anything Hispanic, a later prejudice by Americans, based on their conflict over slavery, resulted in a neglect of African history and culture in the American educational curriculum. Thus, ignorance of African accomplishments has led to disbelief that an African could achieve a geographical *coup*. Thank goodness for Spanish records, Navajo (Diné) myths, American Indian petroglyphs and paintings, Mandinka inscriptions and African ELEPHANTS!

This Flora Vista, New Mexico, Elephant Slab's Public Domain photograph was originally photographed at the now dissolved Gila Pueblo Archeological Foundation in Arizona prior to 1950. Its existence proves that some literate Mali person did visit the Southwest.

Yes,

*They're wanting me, they're haunting
me,*
The awful lonely places;
They're whining and they're whimpering
As if each had a soul;
They're calling from the wilderness,

And now they're all a-crying,
And it's no use me denying;
The spell of them is on me
And I'm helpless as a child;
My heart is aching, aching,
But I hear them, sleeping, waking;
It's the Lure of Little Voices,
It's the mandate of the Wild.

There's a whisper in the night wind,
There's a star agleam to guide us,
And the wild is calling . . . let us go."

Robert W. Service, "The Lure of Little Voices"

1

An Exploration of the North American Southwest before the Arrival of the Spanish

The Society for American Archaeology held a symposium at Santa Fe, New Mexico, in May 1968, to discuss the problems of pre-Columbian contact between the continents and concluded: *"Surely there cannot now be any question but that there were visitors to the New World from the Old in historic or even prehistoric time before 1492."*

According to the abstract of Columbus's log made by Bartolomé de las Casas, the purpose of Columbus's third voyage was to test the claim of King John II of Portugal that "canoes had been found which set out from the coast of Guinea [West Africa] and sailed to the west with merchandise". Also on Columbus' mind was the claim of the native inhabitants of the Caribbean island of Hispaniola that "from the south and the southeast had come black people whose spears were made of an alloyed metal called *guanín* ... from which it was found that of 32 parts: 18 were gold, 6 were silver, and 8 copper"[2], said to be similar to a West African gold alloy. Could these claims be true?

How could "canoes" of West African fabrication possibly have had contact with peoples of "the unknown land" to the west of the Atlantic Ocean? What were the wondrous mechanisms that would have propelled them thither? The answer is prevailing winds and currents—rivers above and in the sea. The Canaries, North Equatorial and Antilles Currents would have brought them to the Caribbean islands, then they, as explorers and traders, would have sailed and rowed their way up and down the Atlantic, Caribbean and Gulf of Mexico coasts, entering the mouths of promising rivers and exploring the interior of the new lands—new to them but old to the native Americans that they encountered. The next question is, *who?* That question, as far as the North American Southwest is concerned, will be answered in this historical *exposé* of one of the most remarkable and unheralded journeys of all time.

Travel Will Resolve

A Jeli/*Griot* saying that may apply to Abu Bakr II: *"What sitting will not solve, travel will resolve...."*

As he made his way to the port, it must have been a stately imperial procession for the golden skullcap crowned "King of Kings" seated on his comfortable litter throne, and shaded by his golden falcon topped silk parasol (based on Ibn Battuta's description and Cresques Abraham's public domain illustration above).

Abu Bakr II's saga is one of probable lengthy adventure on the high seas and one of trial and tribulation in the deserts and valleys of Southwestern North America. As an explorer, he exhibited an unprecedented thirst for geographical knowledge beyond his African empire. His extensive travels indicate a deep desire to circumnavigate the world, not just to reach the western shore of the Atlantic Ocean, as his successor suggested.

It is said that in 1311 Abu Bakr II set out with his Mali Empire fleet of 2000 ships down the Senegal River and sailed out into the Atlantic Ocean. Having set sail westward, leaving his relative Musa to act as Regent of Mali, the Emperor undoubtedly expected to return with good news about the never-before-seen exotic parts of the "unknown world"—but he also must have realized that HE MIGHT NEVER RETURN given the obvious problems of survival at sea. For over seven hundred years it has been a colossal mystery as to what happened to Abu Bakr II and his 2000 ships. That he sailed west toward an "unknown land" was a fact, but his fate also was unknown. Therefore he became the "Mysterious Explorer". People wondered if he had succumbed to Atlantic storms, or washed up on a strange shore, or succeeded in his quest to explore the unknown western "bank" of the Atlantic. No one has had even an inkling of his adventures, although some have speculated that he ended up in South America based on inscriptions found there.

Without a doubt, Abu Bakr II sailed in a style befitting a *Mansa* or "King of Kings". He probably commanded the very best ship, most skilled sailors, most loyal servants, and fiercest warriors. It was said that on the deck of one ship was placed a throne, covered by a royal parasol. A drummer was stationed nearby so the words of the king could fly from ship to ship.

The new fleet of *Mansa* Abu Bakr II was paid for with gold from the Bure, Bambouk, and other mines—and the toil of thousands of subjects. Ready were his best sailors, ship carpenters, navigators, elephant handlers, camel drivers, captains and cooks. The ships this time would carry colonists and trade goods, such as cowrie shells—just in case there was a need to establish a settlement or trade with local people.

According to Egyptian official, Ibn Amir Hajib, the blazon of Emperor Musa was yellow on a red background and standards were unfurled over him wherever he rode his horse—they were very large flags. One has to ask: Did Abu Bakr II also demand this large yellow and red ostentatious exhibition of flags across the Atlantic Ocean? If he did, the flags also might have served as guidons that other ships could focus on to enable them to remain in formation.

Advertisement image for Cheryl Patrice Derricotte, "Ghosts/Ships", Museum of African Diaspora, January 28, 2016 reception and artist talk. Advertisement image is in the public domain.

Who knows how eventful (or uneventful) that voyage might have been? *Mansa* Abu Bakr II would have taken advantage of the information brought back by the only surviving ship from the previous flotilla and either avoided or used the "river at sea". Star patterns, moon phases and magnetic compasses, as well as birds would have been useful too. Birds were used in two major ways. Captive birds, like those mentioned in the Atram-Hasis (a Sumerian king with a round ark), Epic of Gilgamesh and Biblical Noah myths, which did not return if they found land, and those which were used in calculations of distance to land depending on the type of bird (albatross, sea gull, frigate, etc.) and on how far they were seen out to sea from the coast, as well as which direction they were going when they disappeared at sundown. For instance, Polynesians sailing between islands in the Pacific Ocean knew that a species of white tern could be seen up to 120 miles away from their home island, aiding Polynesian navigators in their "way-finding" sailings. A Hawaiian sailor has stated that "way-finding" is a process of using all natural clues all the time. One becomes the wave.

So, perhaps with all of these and other navigational aids, it really was an uneventful crossing, but probably not. For instance:

> Gottlieb Mittelburger, a German who crossed the Atlantic Ocean in 1750 would never forget the terrible misery, stench, fumes, horror, vomiting, many kinds of sickness, fever, dysentery, headache, heat, constipation, boils, scurvy, cancer, mouth-rot and the like, but most of all he remembered the lice. They fed

on everybody, but especially the sick burrowing into their bodies and clothes and spreading disease as they moved from the dying to the living."[24]

After a year with no news from *Mansa* Abu Bakr II, Musa declared himself the new *"Mansa"* and in 1324 CE, set out with 60,000 men in a camel caravan pilgrimage (Al Hajj) to Mecca. *Mansa* Musa gave away so much gold and bought so much cloth, garments, singing girls, and so many Ethiopian and Turkish slave girls in Egypt that the economy there was affected for many years to come. Fortunately, he was interviewed by an Egyptian official and scholars concerning his rise to power. I say fortunately because it has provided us with the only written account of that heroic voyage into the little known ocean by his predecessor.

It is interesting to note the difference between the two traveling emperors—Abu Bakr II and Musa. One headed west across the broad ocean on a secular quest for geographical knowledge while the other headed east across the broad desert sands on a pilgrimage to Mecca. Yet, both were most likely on missions to achieve personal glory.

For determining latitude, day (by the sun's angle) and night (star positions) astronomical readings by Abu Bakr II's navigators would have been important. Measurements of speed and distance traveled each day would have been tallied by an experienced sailor working a chip log and knotted rope thrown from the stern. The number of evenly spaced knots that were pulled overboard in a given amount of time would indicate the speed that the ship was traveling. A boatswain would have made sure that the sailors accomplished their measuring tasks properly. The Emperor would have wanted precise measurements taken of wave height and intervals too, so he could inform his former geography teacher upon his return to Mali. In the meantime, a sailor in a crow's nest or elevated bow would have been assigned to watch for shorelines of islands or land masses, as well as whales, reefs, sandbars, etc.

It seems likely that the Emperor's flotilla first saw the Caribbean Islands in either 1311 or 1312.[22] Professor Mohammed Hamidullah stated that "... in 1311 Mansa Abubakari II, the brave conqueror abdicated his throne to Mansa Kankan Musa and set sail with 1000 ships, each with a gifts and provisions supply ship attached, arriving at the 'new world', the America's [sic] in 1312."[23] "The Moorish Harem" staff has stated that "It was believed that Abubakari arrived on the other end of the Atlantic in the year 1312." So this author also has chosen 1312 CE as the most likely year.

We finally know the answer to the speculation as to Abu Bakr II's "cruise ship" destination. Where he eventually died is still undetermined, but his steadfast exploration has now come to light, thanks to numerous Spanish records, a Navajo myth, Indian petroglyphs, paintings, *kachinas*, and inscriptions in the American Southwest in one of the languages of the Mali Empire.

On reaching the western shores of the Atlantic Ocean, a profusion of fog and clouds may have greeted the Emperor's flotilla as it floated over the continental shelf. The sailor of the Emperor's flagship taking soundings (depth measurements) would have been suddenly and pleasantly surprised one day when the rope weight of the lead line began to drag along the bottom indicating a rising of the sea floor. It still would have been too deep to worry about running aground, but it would have indicated a higher ocean bottom.

After a month or two at sea, the Emperor's ship would have reached a shore—just not a continental shore. The island they were approaching was probably present-day St. Thomas in the American Virgin Islands, east of Puerto Rico. Chart-makers would have noticed a good bay for replenishing supplies. Other ships of the fleet might have become shipwrecked on rocks, reefs and shoals, like Columbus' *Santa Maria*, but the Emperor's flagship apparently did not.

Needing fresh water, fruits, and seafood such as fish and shellfish, the ships would have stopped at the first Caribbean islands they found, like St. Thomas and the Virgin Islands, home of the Taíno Indians, a portion of the Arawak nation. The Arawak are said to have been "a very gentle culture, they preferred negotiation and commercial exchange to war. Their society was characterized by happiness, friendliness and a highly organized hierarchical, paternal society, and a lack of guile."[107]

The Emperor would have been delighted at the prospect of reaching what he must have thought was the eastern shore of Africa or at least the Asian shore his Arab teacher probably had described to him. Any seasick elephants and camels would have been delighted too.

Arawak (Saladoid culture) aka Taíno Indians of the Caribbean, from https://upload.wikimedia.org/wikipedia/commons/5/57/Tropenmuseum_ Royal_Tropical_Institute_Objectnumber_60008905_Een_groep_Arowak ken_en_Karaiben_in_fe.jpg. Public domain.

After all that time at sea viewing nothing but blue water and rain storms, the Emperor and his people would have been overcome by the sight of lush green hills of volcanic St. Thomas. The highest peak is 1555 feet above sea level. Here would have been fresh water, an exciting prospect after weeks of consuming casks of once fresh African water, but by then putrid, stinking remnants. A verdant forest of fruit trees would have provided delightful fresh pulp for the cooks to include in their concoctions. Many fruits were appetizing in their raw form too. What foods would they have relished? How about cassava (yuca), mango, papaya, guava, passion fruit, genip, soursop, sugar apple and sea grapes, if in season.

Then there were the many new varieties of fish, shellfish and small edible animals that the Taíno hunters/fishermen of St. Thomas probably traded with them—animals such as lizards, like the iguana, and birds, like the brown pelican, heron and sea gull. The crew even would have taken the opportunity to stretch their muscles by going net fishing.

"Fishermen with Nets" 1966 Mali stamp by Claude Haley. Public domain.

The Emperor's "trim and fit" soldiers with their sharp, metal weapons would seem to still be remembered in these islands, even if only made of coconuts and prominently displayed on gift shop shelves in Charlotte Amalie, the capital of St. Thomas. Some of the soldiers would have carried bows and quivers of arrows while others would have manfully brandished long spears with points made of iron or _guanín, a gold alloy (18 parts gold, 6 parts silver and 8 parts copper)._

(left) St. Thomas gift shop coconut sculpture of an African warrior with shield and spear, photograph courtesy of Alicia Stanton; and (right) a Fulup warrior near the Senegal River by Friedrich Wilhelm Goedsche of Meissen, 1840, Full peoples gallery in images of all nations. Public domain.

How do we know this—because Christopher Columbus collected some of these golden alloy spear points from Hispaniola's Indians and had the spear points sent back to Spain on a messenger ship, where they were assayed? The results are said to have resembled the gold/silver/copper alloy of West Africa.

(above) _guanín del cacique_ [gold of the chief], and (below) posed native men with head bands, spears, bows and paddle. Images are in the public domain.

14

Taíno Homes. Photograph by Cheyenne Fox Tree McGrath, from http://nativeamericanresources.blogspot.com/2008/02/homes.html. No copyright listed. Photograph is in the public domain.

In addition, in "Analysis of the Hull Bay Skeletons, St. Thomas", *Journal of the Virgin Island Archaeological Society*, 3: 7-14, 1976, Douglas H. Ubelaker and J. Lawrence Angel of The Smithsonian Institution discuss the recovery of skeletons on St. Thomas in 1974 which exhibited Negroid adult male features. Stratigraphy and a nearby pottery fragment may date back to the Elenoid period of pottery design—to 950-1250+ CE. Pottery fragments still could have been present after 1300. Were these two thirty-some year old males, with severe dental diseases, part of the Emperor's fleet? No other burial goods were found to either prove it or disprove it. What these two Negroid skeletons had in common, was possibly a disease called scurvy which causes gum disease and loss of teeth—a common ailment of early sailors and others who did not have sufficient vitamin C in their diet. If these Negroid males were part of the Emperor's crew, then they did not know what Arab sailors and even Columbus knew—that eating onions could prevent this disease. One wonders how many others in the Emperor's entourage had to suffer unnecessarily. The British later discovered that cranberries, limes and other citrus fruits also could be useful—thus the term "limeys" for British sailors.

Vasco Núñez de Balboa, while crossing the Isthmus of Panama (Darien) to the Pacific Ocean in 1513, said that he had seen Black warriors being held as captives of one of the Darien Indian tribes, indicating that some of the Emperor's ships might have gone astray and taken a more southerly route after probably stopping at one of the islands or the mainland for restocking. Monument inscriptions in Brazil indicate that the fleet might have been split up—some ships evidently ascending the eastward flowing Amazon River.

But the Emperor himself probably took a more northerly route across the Puerto Rico Trench, Old Bahama Channel and the Straits of Florida, and would not have been satisfied with just "island hopping" along the northern coasts of Puerto Rico, Hispaniola and Cuba (Columbus supposedly "found on the coast of Cuba dogs that do not bark. This is a West-African race of dogs."). The Emperor had something grander in mind—so they would have sailed on across the Gulf of Mexico. As the restocked ships slowly approached the mainland of the "Unknown Land", the lookouts would have been instructed to keep an eye out for cities, seaports or large river mouths. Finally after inspecting the coastline of Mexico and southern Texas for several days or weeks for an eastward flowing river, one of the lookouts surely would have spotted what looked like the best river mouth available. The Emperor and his advisors probably agreed that this sandy beach with its strong flowing river coming from a deep, grassy, inviting interior was the ideal landing site, or perhaps he made the decision all by himself. Indeed it would have looked like the *"Rio Grande"* that they had been hoping for, probably not unlike the Gambia or Senegal River mouths with which they were so familiar.

Rio Grande by B575 - Own work, CC BY-SA 3.0, Wikimedia Commons. Photograph is in the public domain.

This verdant valley stretching far inland would have appeared to be the most suitable for a penetrating exploration—more so than any of the Caribbean island valleys they had peered into thus far. This author has concluded that given the location of the only evidence yet found, the best route for the expedition would have been to follow the Rio Grande westward and northwestward.

Surely there would be enough water to float smaller, flat bottomed pirogues of West African design, as well as abundant vegetation for the pack and specialty elephants. These would have included elephants for towing boats upstream against strong currents, through rapids, and even to "portage" them around falls and between river systems. Narrow gorges, however, might still pose a few problems. Other elephants, no doubt, were reserved for the Emperor's relatives' and top advisors' luxurious ride. Then there were the fighting elephants—a well-trained war elephant could annihilate any foe.

War-elephants at the Battle of Zama by Henri-Paul Motte, 1890. Picture is in the public domain.

Elephants on Board

Among the "supplies", of course, were camels for possible desert travel and African elephants, for how could one properly go exploring without them? The Emperor's own personal imperial elephant, no doubt, also would have been a passenger on the finest supply ship. In India, a king's elephant keeper had working under him physicians, trainers, riders, foot-chainers, stall-guards, and other attendants. Wouldn't an African emperor have had similar workers, especially onboard a ship? Of course the elephants would have had to have been chained to the ship to prevent movement, but they would also have had to have room to lie down on their sides to prevent suffocation while asleep. The question as to whether elephants could be carried long distances in African designed ships was answered by Ivan Van Sertima who stated that "The Swahili transhipped an elephant to China in the thirteenth century."[21] Lincoln Paine, on page 150 of his book *The Sea and Civilization: A Maritime History of the World,* stated there were even references to "elephant carriers" (*elephantegos*) in classical sources.

Unknown subject with young elephant onboard a ship. When it came to transporting elephants by ship, it is said that young ones were preferred because they ate less. From circa1860's photograph in the public domain.

Despite naysayers who claim that the Emperor's ships could not have transported enough fodder and water to keep elephants alive on a trans-Atlantic voyage, there is abundant proof that it was possible for small ships to do it.

The sailing ship "America", captained by Jacob Crowninshield, brought, in perfect health, the first elephant to the new United States of America in 1796. Nathaniel Hawthorne's father Nathaniel kept a log while on board and noted that at the island of St. Helena "... took on board several pumpkins and cabbages, some fresh fish for ship's use, and greens for the elephant." (underlining by author) Then he wrote in large letters: "ELEPHANT ON BOARD". Cathy Earle, an author, wrote: "Imagine the excitement of the people of New York way back on this date in 1796, when they heard that an Indian elephant had arrived by ship from Calcutta, India." From Kathleen Earle, "April 13—First Elephant Arrives in the U.S.!" Every Day Is Special website, April 13, 2014. In the very early 1800's, other ships brought even more elephants to America.

It doesn't seem likely that there would have been more than one elephant per each of the Emperor's small supply ships. Can you imagine what would have happened if two (or more) elephants started fighting on such small ships? Or what a mess there would have been if two (or more) got seasick? I'm sure that the quartermaster would have foreseen those possibilities and prepared for them; after all, it's not as if there weren't going to be enough ships—for elephants, water and food!

(left) Loading/unloading elephants using slings. Brodie Collection, La Trobe Picture Collection, State Library of Victoria. (right) Image based on "Four ton elephant being unloaded", 1917-1934 (approximate), Courtesy of the Boston Public Library, Leslie Jones Collection, photographer, Leslie Jones, 1886-1967 accession # 08_06_000575, Photographs are in the public domain.

The goal? Would it have been just for an "imperial joy ride" around the world? Possibly, but all explorations have secondary goals—this imperial one, undoubtedly, would have been to search for mineral wealth in the form of silver, copper, tin, or even better, GOLD. The Emperor possibly would have wanted both geographical knowledge <u>and</u> valuable minerals; therefore, he most likely would have brought experienced prospectors and miners too, not unlike the Hebrew King Solomon's nautical expeditions to find the gold of Ophir [future book by this author titled *Mystery Mountain*].

The Overland Journey Begins

Upon landing, Abu Bakr II would have dressed up in his most imperial uniform or imperial robes for this momentous occasion. He not only would have wanted to appear authoritative in front of his own people, but impressive to the gawking Native Americans. As he issued direct, forceful and compelling orders on how to safely and efficiently go ashore, his ship captains, quartermasters and military commanders would have quickly and effectively carried them out. Everyone probably was relieved finally to be disembarking and getting far, far away from their cramped and uncomfortable shipboard seats and beds. The crews would have carefully beached or anchored their ships and unloaded men, women and supplies close to shore or into smaller boats. The elephants and any other large animals would have been carefully fitted with slings and swung over the rails into shallow water or onto land. One group of servants, of course, would have been detailed to set up the Emperor's pavilion for his comfort under the boiling sun. As the local residents looked at the gathering of monster beasts and their scurrying servants, it probably never occurred to them to attack the invaders—due partly, no doubt, to the wondrous sight of winged, gigantic canoes, and partly to the overwhelming size of "the monsters" and the army of fierce looking warriors.

It would have been obvious that these warriors from afar and that their "masters"—the gigantic gray beasts—were just too big to successfully resist if they did attack. Best to keep hidden and hope they would merely go away.

(left) Terracotta archer and (center) cavalry figures plus a bronze soldier from Mali (13th -15th century). These sculptures represent soldiers dressed in military gear. They are equipped with quivers (cases to hold arrows) on their backs and knives strapped to each of their left arms. The horse is equipped with a bridle and ceremonial adornment around its neck. (right) Soldier with spear in right hand and shield under left arm— bearded with protruding eyes, (lost wax cast bronze, found buried near the Niger River in Mali). Early Arabic documents attest to the importance of the court's cavalry and describe riders wearing wide-legged pants, close-fitting caps and anklets and carrying quivers. Mansa Musa's army was reported to have been 100,000 strong and his cavalry composed of 10,000 men. How many his predecessor, Mansa Abu Bakr II, took with him is unknown. From Smithsonian's Mali Empire and Djenne figures, Works of Art, website; photographs by Franko Khoury. These photographs are in the public domain since (left & center) they were taken by a government employee and (right) an unknown photographer.

It also would have been obvious to the newcomers that the coast held not a speck of the mineral wealth that they sought, so they would have assembled their caravan of strong elephants, and flotilla of flat-bottomed river boats, once used months before on the Gambia and Senegal Rivers of West Africa, and proceeded westward up the "Grand River" of the unknown land (which the delighted Emperor from his elevated mobile throne might have considered his "New Mali").

Carthaginian *shekel* with a man riding an elephant dated 237-227 BCE. This image is in the public domain

A Mandinka proverb states: "The hunter in pursuit of an elephant does not stop to throw stones at birds", meaning don't waste time when pursuing your dream. The Emperor's crew was undoubtedly reminded of this by *Mansa* Abu Bakr from time to time. The crew would have responded "*Mansa Abu Bakr Ki*"—meaning "Emperor Abu Bakr has commanded".

24

"On the average the Rio Grande Plain, neglecting its local irregularities, slopes toward the Gulf at the rate of about 5 feet to the mile"[25] The caravan of elephants, camels and river boats, therefore, started ascending the valley and river at the rate of about 5 feet per mile. This average rate of ascent for the journey as far as the mouth of the Rio Chama near Ohkay Owingeh Pueblo would have been a very suitable pace for large animals and servants on foot. Some obstacles, like the Big Bend in Texas, La Bajada volcanic cliff and the Continental Divide in New Mexico would have presented problems, but were not insurmountable. The canyons in Utah and Arizona as well as the lack of adequate grasses and brush for the elephants in Arizona, however, were problems that became formidable challenges for the Emperor's party. Nevertheless, there were no insurmountable obstacles that would have forced the Emperor to turn his caravan around and return to the Gulf of Mexico where he had disembarked. The Emperor, of course, would have left a colony of Mali men and women at the Rio Grande's mouth—marine warriors to guard and sailors and ship carpenters to repair his ships, as well as women and girls using pots and cauldrons to feed the crews in their camp, just in case he was forced to 'give up his dream of circumnavigating the gourd-like world.

Camp cooking in Koulikoro, Mali on the banks of The Niger River. Photograph from http://natashaoxenburgh.blogspot.com/2010/04/girls-camp.html. No copyright listed.

The Texas State Historical Association claims that in the Rio Grande Delta, the Brownsville Complex is unique for its trade with frontier Mesoamerican cultures (e.g., the Huastecs of Veracruz), which took place around 1300–1400 CE. Members of the Brownsville Complex made shell beads and other ornaments in large numbers and traded these to the Huastecs in return for pottery vessels, jadeite ornaments, and glass-like obsidian, all found in Brownsville Complex sites in the lower Rio Grande Valley. It has been said that not much is known about the antecedents of the curious Brownsville Complex, perhaps with good reason. Their ancestors may have been in Africa, not North America or Asia.

Obsidian trade items became sharp arrow points, scrappers, knives etc.

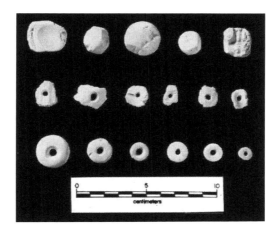

"Shell-bead Making: The manufacture of round shell beads starts with "blanks," pieces of shell that have been broken or slightly rounded, such as the objects on the top row. On the middle row are roughed-out shell beads with drilled holes for suspension onto a necklace strand. Once the drilled beads were ground flat, they were tightly strung and the edges were ground and smoothed, strand-by-strand, creating uniform beads." From http://texasbeyondhistory.net/ brownsville/index.html. This image is in the public domain.

According to Alvise Cadamosto (circa 1432 – July 16, 1483),[26] an Italian slave trader and explorer who was hired by the Portuguese Prince Henry the Navigator:

27

Mali marines wore white caps on their heads and a white tunic. On the side of the skullcaps worn by the Malian marines, a white wing decoration was emblaxoned (sic), and a feather was stuck in the middle of the skull cap.[27] On board each naval vessel stood a marine with a round leather shield on the arm and a short sword. Other marines were armed with bows and arrows.

Chuma, David Livingstone's servant, of the Yao tribe, with bow and arrow. Note the feather in the hair. Image is from Wikipedia "Chuma and Susi". Public domain

It has been:

reported that the Malian military wore a uniform consisting of sandles (sic), loose fitting cotton breeches reaching down to the knees, a sleeveless tunic, and a white headdress of either cotton or leather, decorated with one or more feathers. The major weapons of the Malian soldier included iron-pointed spears, daggers and short swords, wooden battle-clubs and the bow and arrow.[28]

Spanish Capitán Carlos Cantú Finds a Community of Well-Armed Blacks

It is said that the first of the Spanish colonizers and explorers of the Rio Grande Valley later reported a group of Blacks on the lower stretches of the Rio Grande, in a place within the present city of Brownsville.

> Captain Carlos Cantú, who had earlier led a group of Spanish colonists from Nuevo León in 1749, came across a colony of blacks on a river island in the braided lower Rio Grande. Speculation on the origin of the people, noted as being independent and well armed, was wide ranging. They were called escapees from earlier slave ships or stranded mariners or were simply left unexplained, like the blacks seen in present-day Panama before Balboa. That they preceded the Spanish to the area is known ... [29]

It is not conceivable that this "independent and well-armed" group could have been escaped slaves or sailors. The Texas community of Blacks [this author believes to be most likely descendants of fourteenth century Mali explorers], "apparently quite durable, was identifiable until the nineteenth century".[29] It would not be unreasonable to assume that, once discovered, these descendants of the Mali sailors, marines, cooks, etc. were eventually overcome by Spanish slavers and that survivors ended up working as slaves in Mexican silver mines. Another mystery of a Spanish record solved.

"Mining in Potosí", Peru, an engraving from Theodoor de Bry in *Historia Americae sive Novi Orbis.* This image is in the public domain.

Indian Encounters

Abu Bakr II would have sent out exploratory expeditions up each promising tributary and visible high hill, and into each side canyon, but probably the results were always disappointing. His imperial prospectors, of course, would have failed to uncover even one nugget in southern Texas or northern Mexico. Abu Bakr II would have been irritated at the poor showing, but he was adventurous and part of his desire to explore the far shores of the ocean (or possibly to circumnavigate the globe) was to satisfy his curiosity. He wasn't yet fully satisfied, so onward he traveled to find the Western shore, not realizing how far away it really was, or how sparse healthy fodder for the elephants would become.

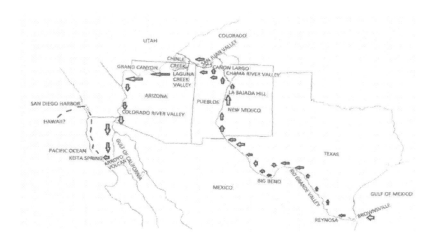

Map of the North American Southwest showing route (arrows) of Emperor Abu Bakr II's caravan east to west. Dashed line indicates the most likely route to a harbor with trees where a new fleet of ships could be constructed and sailed westward. Map created by Ronald Stewart.

Day after day, the imperial caravan would have carefully and slowly trudged ever westward, but following the bends in the river as they swerved in one direction or another. As they climbed uphill, the intrepid explorers would have noticed that the vegetation changed considerably. New species of plant-life would have appeared—plants unknown in Western Africa such as small barrel cactus, honey mesquite, Texas ebony and Texas *huisache* (sweet acacia). The interlopers quickly would have discovered that despite their bright orange and yellow flowers, Texas *lantera* was poisonous to grazing animals. Elephants still would have had grass and brush enough to eat, but special care had to be taken as to where the elephants grazed. Which new flora might be poisonous to them would have been difficult to ascertain. The handlers (or elephant servants) probably had to rely on their elephants' natural instincts for avoiding those plants. Nevertheless, the handlers would have had to constantly watch for any sign of sickness.

Although no African cobras, or vipers, were sighted, possibly the bite of an occasional rattlesnake was felt. As far as vicious animals, none in their right mind, unless rabid, would have dared to attack an elephant—not even a *lobo* (wolf), which probably could be heard frequently at night. Because of the daytime encounters with prairie dogs, deer and pronghorns, it would have been reassuring that edible grasses were available.

As settlements were encountered, probably residents at first fled, but this might have changed as word spread from camp to camp that these visitors were more interested in trade and mining than conquest or theft. The Emperor probably kept discipline strict, so few native residents were harmed—a gesture that would not have been lost on the natives. This, of course, would result in better trades and increased amounts of fresh pronghorn and deer meat and something that tasted like rich jerky meat. However, considerable time probably passed before bison were actually seen on the hoof.

Buffalo silhouetted against a Texas sunset. Photo courtesy of Texas Parks and Wildlife Department. This image is in the public domain.

The Carrizo/Comecrudo tribe would have been one of the first people encountered. They referred to themselves as "Esto'k gna", who revered the bison, or "*wakate*", as they called it.[30]

The Carrizo/Comecrudo (Esto'k gna) people lived along the South Texas Rio Grande delta. The records for their existence are scarce. The earliest documentation found on the Comecrudo is in the Spaniard, Count of Sierra, José de Escandón's interesting account of his reconnaissance of 1747 CE. Escandón's main source of information on Native Americans of the Rio Grande delta came from a Comecrudo leader, Capitan Santiago, who was clearly the acknowledged leader of other Native American groups of the area. Capitan Santiago summoned other Native Americans by use of smoke signals, and some two hundred Indian families came to the locality of Escandón's camp. Escandón obtained from Capitan Santiago the native names of thirty Native American groups said to be living along the lower Rio Grande, sixteen groups south of the river and fourteen north of it. The Comecrudos were apparently more numerous than other Native American groups of the Rio Grande delta and seemed to have lived very near the Gulf coast of the river *Ahamatau Mete'l pase'l*, meaning "river of spirit life". Did Abu Bakr II's sudden arrival at the mouth of the Rio Grande bring about another general meeting of the bands back in 1312 CE?

These Native Americans lived in reed huts and claimed to speak the oldest language in Texas. Many small autonomous bands with little political unity above the level of the band inhabited the lands surrounding the lower Rio Grande River. One scholar thought that they "represent the culmination of more than 11,000 years of a way of life that had successfully adapted to the climate and resources of south Texas."[31] They shared the common traits of being non-agricultural. They were nomadic hunter-gatherers, carrying their meager possessions on their backs as they moved from place to place to exploit sources of food that might be available only seasonally. At each campsite, they built small circular huts with frames of four bent poles which they covered with woven mats. They wore little clothing. At times, they came together in large groups of several bands and hundreds of people, but most of the time their encampments were small, consisting of a few huts and a few dozen people."[32]

"The Coahuiltecans, as the Spanish later collectively named the native Americans of the Rio Grande country, had good bows and arrows and hunted small game. Occasionally bison strayed into their region from the Great Plains to the north. They also subsisted, during times of need, on worms, lizards, ants, and undigested seeds collected from deer dung. They ate much of their food raw, but used an open fire or a fire pit for cooking. Most of their food came from plants. Pecans were an important food, gathered in the fall and stored for future use. In summer, large numbers of people congregated at the vast thickets of prickly pear cactus south-east of [present-day] San Antonio where they feasted on the fruit and the pads and interacted socially with other bands. They cooked the bulbs and root crowns of the *maguey, sotol,* and *lechuguilla* in pits and made flour out of *mesquite beans.*"[33] Most of the Coahuiltecans seem to have had a regular round of travels in search of food.

"The Payaya band near San Antonio had ten different summer campsites in an area 30 miles square. Some of the Indians lived near the coast in winter and journeyed 85 miles (140 km) inland to exploit the prickly pear cactus thickets in summer."[34] "Fish were perhaps the principal food item for the bands living in the Rio Grande delta."[35]

yellow bullhead (*Ameiurus natalis*) photograph by L .M. Page from
https://www.floridamuseum.ufl.edu/catfish/ictaluridae/yellowbullhead.htm
Public domain.

Robert Abel of San Antonio, Texas, and his record Rio Grande Cichlid
(*Herichthys cyanoguttatus*) aka Rio Grande Perch. Public domain.

It has been said that "... Coahuiltecans ... came together in large numbers on occasion for all-night dances called *mitotes* in which **peyote** was eaten to achieve a trance-like state. The meager resources of their homeland led to intense competition and frequent, although small scale, warfare."[36]

Flowering peyote plants, photograph in public domain.

1890 Illustration of a Coahuilteco man by Frank Weir. public domain.

The Big Bend is named for the vast curve of the Rio Grande in southwest Texas. It is a wildly beautiful natural region. The Emperor's caravan eventually entered and traversed the Big Bend of the Rio Grande, no doubt exploring and enjoying the pictographs that are visible along the cliff wall. Local Indians painted these with a bright, reddish, mineral and may have even shown the Emperor's prospectors the outcroppings of this cinnabar (from which the liquid metal mercury is extracted). The Emperor and elite members of his party probably also soaked in the 105°F water that bubbles up from a hole in the ground. Known today as Hot Springs (near Tornillo Creek) these curative warm waters were eventually turned into a 21 day treatment of bathing and drinking spring water by homesteaders J.O. and Bessie Langford in 1909. Other Rio Grande obstacles that the Emperor's Caravan might have had to overcome included Tight Squeeze Rapids, Black Dike, and Rock Slide Rapids. Black Dike is named for the volcanic dike that crosses the river. Forces that raised the Chisos Mountains through thousands of feet of sedimentary rock are evident at Black Dike where a finger of magma (called a dike) once forced itself through softer rock while in a molten state. That softer rock has now eroded away, leaving the dark colored basalt standing alone. Near today's community or ghost town of Terlingua is a possible petroglyph of an elephant—perhaps the first elephant petroglyph indicating the route of the "Abu Bakr II trail".

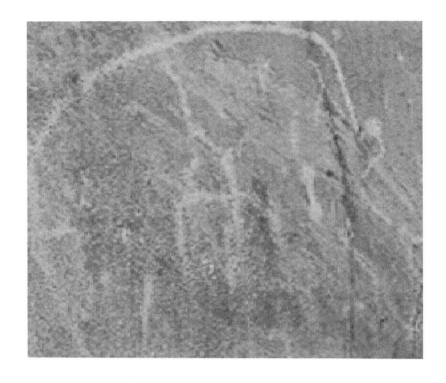

Possible petroglyph of an elephant in Big Bend National Park near Terlingua, Texas. Public domain photograph.

The Rio Grande's Tight Squeeze Rapids in Big Bend National Park.
Photograph courtesy of the National Park Service. Public domain.

The Rio Grande's Black Dike in Big Bend National Park from Earlham College Physical Geology 2002 website. Public domain.

Rio Grande's Rock Slide Rapids in Big Bend National Park. Public domain.

Beyond the Coahuiltecan bands, the Chizo band of the Concho Indians occupied the valley where the Concho River of Mexico joins the Rio Grande at La Junta, and just north of them were their friends, the Jumanos. Antonio de Espejo named them Abriaches and Otomoacas in 1583. The Chizos farmed, gathered and hunted, especially deer, rabbits and birds. They also fished in the rivers with nets, and used pits, snares and traps to ensnare small animals.

The locations and Spanish names of Indian bands in western Texas and adjacent Mexico, circa 1600. Map by Smallchief is in the public domain. From Wikimedia Commons.

An imagined hide covered hut of a pre-historic Texas Indian family, at the Nightengale Archeological Center, Kingsland, Texas, based on circles of stones found near creeks and lakes; photograph in public domain.

The next people that the Emperor would have encountered were called Suma, but Antonio de Espejo later called them Caguates. Early visitors declared that the Suma "are hunters; they eat all sorts of game, wild reptiles, and acorns ... mesquite beans, tunas and other cactus fruits, roots, seeds, and unspecific game animals. They have no knowledge whatsoever of agriculture, have no fixed homes, or ranches, and live a carefree life."[38]

After traveling west and northwest, Abu Bakr II would have been surprised by the gradual turn that the big river (Rio Grande) took to the north and even northeast after it passed by the Franklin Mountains, but sensing no real advantage to continuing westward across waterless desert, he would have chosen the obvious northward, well-watered and grassy route—besides the valley is where most of the native peoples lived. Some of these peoples were the non-agricultural

Indians called Tampachoas by Antonio de Espejo in 1583, who stated: "We found a great number of people living near some lagoons through the midst of which the Rio del Norte [Rio Grande] flows. These people, who must have numbered more than a thousand men and women, and who were settled in their *rancherias* and grass huts, came out to receive us.... Each one brought us his present of mesquite bean ... fish of many kinds, which are very plentiful in these lagoons, and other kinds of food ... During the three days and nights we were there they continually performed ... dances in their fashion, as well as after the manner of the Mexicans."[39] Espejo's Tampachoas were probably the same people whom Juan de Oñate found in the same area fifteen years later in May 1598 and called Mansos. Oñate and his large expedition forded the Rio Grande near Socorro, Texas assisted by 40 "manxo" Indians. Manso meant "gentle" or "docile" in Spanish. Their name for themselves is unknown.[39] In 1630, a Spanish priest described the Mansos as people "who do not have houses, but rather pole structures. Nor do they sow; they do not dress in anything particular; but all are nude and only the women cover themselves from the waist down with deerskins." In 1663, a Spaniard said of them, "The nation of Manso Indians is so barbarous and uncultivated that all its members go naked and, although the country is very cold, they have no houses in which to dwell, but live under the trees, not even knowing how to till the land for their food." The Mansos were also said to eat fish and meat raw. But they were described somewhat favorably as "a robust people, tall, and with good features, although they take pride in bedaubing themselves with powder of different colors which makes them look very ferocious."[39]

45

Traveling up the Rio Grande Valley from the southeast, these intrepid African explorers, like their successors the Spanish explorers in the colonial period, viewed two mountain ranges rising out of the desert with a deep chasm between. The river passed through the chasm. The Spanish named the site El Paso del Norte (the Pass of the North) which became the site of Ciudad Juárez, Mexico, and El Paso, Texas. More mountains soon came into view to the east and west, so prospectors would have been quickly dispatched. The Organ Mountain prospectors might have revealed that the northern edge of the mountain wilderness had high mineral resource potential for copper, silver, and gold and the western edge had moderate resource potential for lead, zinc, copper, silver and gold—all worthwhile minerals.[40]

Northernmost peaks of the Organ Mountains called "The Needles". Public domain.

However, the Black Range showed tin deposits, while the future Santa Rita area yielded copper and the future Silver City region gold, silver and zinc deposits.[41] Finally, the Emperor might have thought: I have reason to hope my new empire, if I have to remain here, will pay off. After studying the prospectors' promising reports, including possibly their discovery, on a side trip to the east, of a small desert of white gypsum sands. If indeed the future White Sands National Monument was explored, the caravan probably was ordered to avoid the beautiful, but treacherous, sands and proceed up the Rio Grande Valley where there was adequate vegetation for his elephants and hunting for his caravan members.

One day, some of Abu Bakr II's scouts probably rushed back down the Rio Grande Valley to the Emperor's northward bound caravan with wonderful news. The Emperor would have seen from their excitement that they must have discovered something truly fantastic. Was it gold, he possibly wondered, or was it signs of the next ocean shore for which he was so desperately searching. He knew that his caravan was far above sea level, so he would have quickly put that thought out of his mind. But their news did involve a different kind of water. Water that a dusty, sweaty, bug bitten emperor would relish, just as the Southwestern hunters, gatherers, Mimbres Indians, and Piro speaking pueblo Indians must have in the past, and Apaches, Spanish and Americans would enjoy some centuries later.

Tumble Inn Mud Baths in Hot Springs Cure Rheumatism, from sierracountynewmexico.info. Public domain.

What lay in the Emperor's path? What couldn't his caravan avoid? Water! And the water was hot! At a river bend not far ahead lay marshy springs and pools of pleasingly hot and warm waters, plus a swampy basin of warm mud, subject to seasonal flooding from the Rio Grande. It was the site of the later Truth or Consequences community, once named Palomas Hot Springs or just Hot Springs, New Mexico. The Emperor probably would have been overjoyed. Without a doubt, he and his elite fellow travelers would have soaked, sometimes laying in the hot mud and slathering it all over themselves while other times enjoying themselves by splashing and relaxing in other pools to their hearts' content. Servants and slaves may have had to make do with the cooler waters of the Rio Grande below the hot springs.

The earliest known photo of mud-slathered people enjoying the health benefits of hot springs. This photograph is thought to be from the 1860's or 1870's. The photo shows that therapeutic benefits of the Hot Springs were thought to exist several centuries ago. Photo courtesy of Truth or Consequences Chamber of Commerce. Public domain.

The hot thermal water unexpectedly issues from a rift along the Rio Grande that was created more than 50 million years ago. The rift uplifted a hill and opened faults along the rift to allow deep groundwater to flow freely to the surface without losing heat or minerals. This produced pristine waters with temperatures ranging from 98 to 115 degrees, with trace elements of 38 different minerals. According to a Charles Motel & Spa mineral water analysis, minerals included:[42]

Element		ppm		Element		ppm
Ag	Silver	0.001		Li	Lithium	1.300
Al	Aluminum	0.050		Mg	Magnesium	15.300
Ar	Arsenic	0.050		Mn	Manganese	0.010
Au	Gold	0.005		Mo	Molybdenum	0.002
B	Boron	0.250		Na	Sodium	751.000
Ba	Barium	0.200		Ni	Nickel	0.002
Br	Bromine	2.600		Pb	Lead	0.002
Ca	Calcium	163.000		Rb	Rubidium	0.700
Cd	Cadmium	0.001		Sb	Antimony	0.050
Cl	Chloride	1360.000		Se	Selium	0.050
Co	Cobalt	0.001		Si	Silicon	21.000
Cr	Chromium	0.002		Sr	Strontium	3.820
Cs	Cesium	0.120		Hg	Mercury	0.050
Cu	Copper	0.002		K	Potassium	56.000
F	Floride	3.060		U	Uranium	0.100
Fe	Iron	0.020		Zn	Zinc	0.010

Compound		ppm
HCO_3	Bicarbonate	220.000
NH_4	Ammonium	0.050
NO_3	Nitrate	0.200
PO_4	Phosphate	0.200
SiO_2	Silicate	45.000
SO_4	Sulfate	75.100

How would the Emperor have played in these hot waters? His actions probably would not have differed much from this author's thoroughly enjoyable soaking experience at the quiet, enchanting hot springs refuge, at the river's bend, overlooking Turtleback Mountain—except for whatever Mali imperial protocol or ceremony had to be followed.

Passing the large rock known to water sports enthusiasts today as "Elephant Butte" (site of New Mexico's largest man-made lake) the surprised Emperor possibly would have considered this sighting as a very good omen, given his admiration for his caravan of elephants.

Elephant Butte on the Rio Grande in New Mexico. Public domain.

Other sights that would have impressed members of the northward bound caravan would have included Nogal Canyon; 10,141 foot high San Mateo peak to the west of them in the San Mateo Mountains; Milligan Gulch; Jornada lava flow to the east of the Rio Grande; 10,783 foot high South Baldy and 9,858 foot high North Baldy peaks in the

Magdalena Mountains. Then there were the peaks north of Blue Canyon, such as Socorro, Strawberry and Polvadera, dotting their western view; 9,176 foot Ladron Peak (Spanish for thief), north of Rio Salado (Salty River); and the abundant birds and animals that lived near the waterway (today's Bosque del Apache and Sevilleta National Wildlife Refuges).

Photographs of sandhill cranes and a coyote by Chuanxiao Li. Public domain.

Birds in flight photographed by Chuanxiao Li. Public domain.

51

Next was the Manzano/Sandia mountain chain, where prospectors probably once again failed to uncover anything. The nearby Pueblo Indians had not mined anything but blue-green stones either. Their only other mining interests were in collecting salt, finding good pottery clay and digging *acequias* (irrigation ditches). However, the Emperor possibly would have appreciated the colorful turquoise stones that the Indians traded, strung for necklaces, etc., and although hardly worth a king's ransom, trading for these turquoise rocks might have been brisk and productive.

Since the next riverside natives were Pueblo Indian farmers, probably they would have shared their supplies of the three sisters—corn, beans and squash—and traded for even more such as venison, elk, rabbit and bison meats.

Mule Deer,   Jack Rabbit, and   American Bison in public domain

The first Pueblo Indians the Emperor's caravan would have encountered were Piro speakers, or as they referred to themselves, *At se em*, "The People". "Records estimate some 16,000 members of a well-established group of salt traders who occupied over twelve pueblos along the Rio Grande River"[43] and even more pueblo dwellers known as Tompiros, west of the Estancia saline lakes (Salinas) to the east of Abó Pueblo.

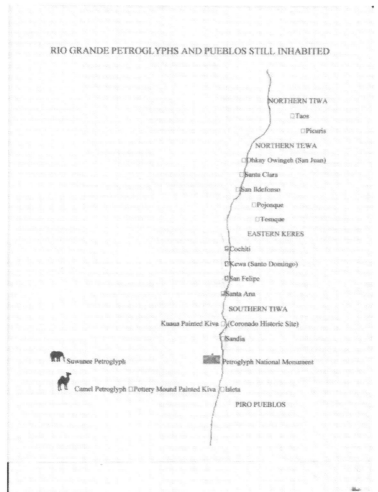

RIO GRANDE PETROGLYPHS AND PUEBLOS STILL INHABITED

NORTHERN TIWA
   ☐Taos
    ☐Picuris

NORTHERN TEWA
☐Ohkay Owingeh (San Juan)
☐Santa Clara
☐San Ildefonso
  ☐Pojoaque
  ☐Tesuque

EASTERN KERES
☐Cochiti
☐Kewa (Santo Domingo)
☐San Felipe
☐Santa Ana

SOUTHERN TIWA
Kuaua Painted Kiva ☐(Coronado Historic Site)
☐Sandia

Suwanee Petroglyph

Petroglyph National Monument

Camel Petroglyph ☐Pottery Mound Painted Kiva ☐Isleta

PIRO PUEBLOS

Rio Grande Pueblo linguistic divisions with present day pueblos [squares], some pueblo ruins, and petroglyph sites that the Emperor's caravan would have passed by on its way north up the Rio Grande Valley. Painted Kiva [underground ceremonial chamber] murals, such as Pottery Mound's and Kuaua's at Coronado Historic Site, Bernalillo, New Mexico, are indicated. The map was drawn by Ronald Stewart.

Cross Section of an Idealized Pueblo

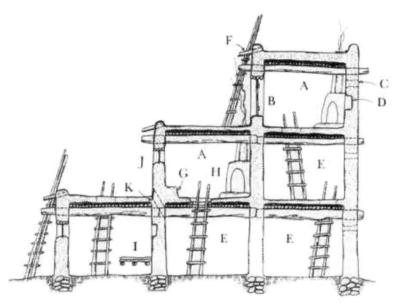

A. Sleeping/Cooking Room, **B** . Door, **C.** Air Vent, **D.** Niche, **E.** Store Room, **F.** Canale (roof drain), **G.** Banco (bench), **H.** Fireplace, **I.** Sleeping Room, **J.** Small Window, **K.** Angled Window

Rising solar heat warms south-facing rooftops, creating outdoor work areas during the winter months. Rooftop entrances provide protection from rattlesnakes, wolves—and attackers. From U.S. Department of the Interior, Bureau of Land Management, Children and Science Articles website. Public domain illustration.

The Indians raised turkeys and cultivated beans and corn for tortillas, and other kinds of bread, but their methods of cultivation and irrigation of crops was said to have been different from that of other Indians to the north. The Emperor's religious leaders possibly would have been fascinated by the subterranean *kivas* used for religious purposes. "Piro Pueblos had two religious groups, which were the clown societies and medicine societies. The clown societies performed two functions: to relieve tensions and to maintain order. The medicine society may have been established as early as 1300 AD. They were the herbal healers and spiritual leaders of each community."[44] The Emperor may have witnessed one *At se em* ceremony.[45] What the Spanish named San Felipe, was the southernmost occupied Piro pueblo in New Mexico, Qualacu was next, then Senecú which was located on the west bank of the Rio Grande opposite Black Mesa. The name of the pueblo was either *Tze-no-que*, *Tzen-o-cue*, or *She-an-ghua*, translated as either "eye socket", or what is more likely "spring hole". Travelers throughout the 18th century reported seeing Senecú's ruins, however, they are not visible anymore. Other Piro pueblos that the Emperor's caravan would have passed included Teypana (where later explorers emerging from an inhospitable desert would be given food and water by the people) and Pilabó (site of present-day Socorro, New Mexico).[46] Piro speaking Pueblos which were noted and named by later Spanish explorers were: Abó (on the Arroyo del Empedradillo, about 25 miles east of the Rio Grande and 20 miles south of Manzano, in Valencia County), Agua Nueva (on the Rio Grande between Socorro and Servilleta), Alamillo (on the east bank of the Rio Grande about 12 miles north of Socorro), Barrancas (on the Rio Grande near Socorro), Qualacu (on the east bank of the Rio Grande near the foot of the Black Mesa, on or near the site of San Marcial, 24 miles south of Socorro), San Felipe (on the west bank of the Rio Grande, probably near Milligan Gulch, about 30 miles south of Socorro), San Pascual (on the east bank of the Rio Grande, opposite the present San Antonio village, 10 miles south of Socorro), Senecu (on the west bank of the Rio Grande, at the site of the present village of San Antonio, 13 miles below Socorro), Seelocu (renamed Sevilleta by Oñate in 1598 because of its location on a bluff overlooking the Rio Guadaquivir (another ancient name given to the Rio Grande) had reminded him of Seville in Spain) (on the east bank of the Rio Grande about 20 miles north of Socorro, between the confluence of the Rio Puerco and Rio Salado with the Rio Grande), Socorro or Pilabo (on the site of the present Socorro, renamed Socorro by the Spanish), Tabira (at the southern apex of the Mesa de los Jumanos, northeast of the present Socorro), Tenabo (probably at the Siete Arroyos, northeast of Socorro and east of the Rio Grande), Teypana (nearly opposite present city of Socorro) and Tenaquel (?). *

---

*Names of deserted pueblos near the lower Rio Grande which were also in all probability occupied by the Piro were: Amo, Aponitre, Aquicabo, Atepua, Ayqui, Calciati, Canocan, Cantensapue, Cunquilipinoy, Encaquiagualcaca, Huertas (4 miles below Peixoloe or Feixoloe, which was on the west side of the Rio Grande), Pencoana, Penjeacd, Pesquis, Peytre, Polooca, Preguey, Pueblo Blanco (on the west rim of the Médano, or great sand-flow, east of the Rio Grande, about lat. 34° 30′), Medano Pueblo, (or great sand-flow, east of the Rio Grande), Pueblo Colorado (same location as Pueblo Blanco), Pueblo de la Parida (same location as Pueblos Blanco and Colorado), Pueblo del Alto (on the east side of the Rio Grande, 6 miles south of Belen), Queelquelu, Quialpo, Quiapo, Quiomaquf, Quiubaco, Tecahanqualahamo, Teeytraan, TercAo, Texa, Teyaxa, Tohol, Trelagf, Trelaquepu, Treyey, Treypual, Trula, Tuzahe, Vumahein, Yancomo, and Zumaque. The following deserted pueblos at the time of Spanish exploration were inhabited either by the Piro or the Tiwa: Acoli Pueblo, Aggey Pueblo, Alle Pueblo, Amaxa Pueblo, Apena Pueblo, Atuyama Pueblo, Axauti Pueblo, Chein Pueblo, Cizentetpl Pueblo, Couna Pueblo, Dhiu Pueblo, Hohota Pueblo, Mejia Pueblo (5 leagues below Isleta), Quanquiz Pueblo, San Bautista Pueblo (on the Rio Grande, 16 miles below Sevilleta), Xatoe Pueblo, Xiamela Pueblo (?), and Yonalus Pueblo.

All the above pueblos not definitely located were probably situated in the Salinas in the vicinity of Abo. (Adapted from https://www.accessgenealogy.com/native/piro-pueblo-indians.htm).

The Emperor's scouts possibly would have reported that San Lorenzo Canyon, between present-day Socorro and Albuquerque, west of the Rio Grande, would be worth seeing. Millions of years of Earth's history unfold in San Lorenzo Canyon, a picturesque area of sandstone cliffs and hoodoos. It features beautiful wild flowers, wild animals, arches, caves, slot canyons, interesting inclusions of minerals, as well as unique and fascinating geological formations. Springs, dry-fall pour-offs and tiny creeks also are hidden in the canyon bottoms and washes. The main cliffs have eroded into interesting sculptures—and even pillars. Hopefully, Abu Bakr II descended from his imperial elephant and "took a hike"—the best way to experience the beauty of this exciting and stimulating landscape.

United States Bureau of Land Management photograph from https://www.blm.gov/visit/san-lorenzo-canyon. Public domain.

The next Pueblo Indians to the north (Albuquerque area) spoke Tiwa (Tigua), one of the Tanoan languages of the Uto-Aztecan family of languages. Some Tiwa Indians were living on the present site of Tue-I (Isleta) and were accomplished weavers of cotton cloth, even making cotton embroidery.

Isleta family, 1890, photo by Charles Lummis; Kate Peck collection, Wheelwright Museum of the American Indian. Public domain.

"Espejo reported that the indigenous men wore shirts and small pieces of colored cotton cloth, and the women wore cotton skirts embroidered with cotton thread. In the same decade, Gallegos wrote of the "painted and embroidered clothing that the southern Tiwa wore,... it is the best that has been found". Castano's report from Pecos (circa 1590 CE) detailed the residents' winter clothing: "We noted that most of the men, if not all, wore cotton blankets and over these a buffalo skin, since this was the cold season; some covered their privy parts with small pieces of cloth, very elegant and elaborately decorated. The women wear a blanket tied over the shoulder and left open on one side, with a sash the width of a span wrapped around the waist. Over this blanket they wear another, nicely decorated and very fancy....."[47]

Others were living in eleven villages at the Pueblos of Moho, aka Piedras Marcadas, ("marked boulders") (west side of Albuquerque), Calabacilas, Chamisal, Puaray and Maigua (both close to Alameda, site of a large Tiwa pueblo located where the Alameda elementary school is today), Corrales (west side), Sandia (east side), Watche, Santiago (Bernalillo), and Kuaua (Coronado Historic Site, west side, north of Bernalillo) which, with the exception of Isleta and Sandia, are just some of these Southern Tiwa speaking pueblos which are ruins or sites of gravel pits, warehouse stores, a school, etc. today.*

---

*The following are the Tigua (Tiwa) pueblos, so far as known:
Presently Inhabited:
Isleta, Picuris (Northern Tiwa), Sandia, and Taos (Northern Tiwa),
Others Uninhabited:
Bejuituuy, Carfaray, Chilili, Lentes, Manzano, Mojualuna, Nabatutuei, Natchurituei, Pahquetooai, Puretuay, Quarai (east of the Manzano Mountains), San Antonio, Shumnac and Tajique.
The following pueblos now extinct, probably were also Tigua:
Acacafui, Guayotrf, Henicohio, Leyva, Paniete, Poxen, Ranchos, Shinana, Tanques, Torreon, Trimati, Tuchiamas and Vareato.
(Adapted from https://www.accessgenealogy.com/native/tigua-pueblo-indians.htm).

The Indians of this region probably couldn't help but be impressed by the ponderous pachyderms, humped camels and the "Black People", but did the native people record the monstrous beasts in rock art, or paint images of these previously unknown god-like people in their Indian ceremonial kivas? Images in and around Pottery Mound Pueblo, on the Rio Puerco, would suggest that they did.

(left) Ronald Stewart's reproduction (legs partially filled in) of a kiva mural from Kiva 8, Pottery Mound on the Rio Puerco, west of Isleta Pueblo, New Mexico. Note the short, black figure (with bulging muscles) rotating in mid air as suggested by the curved lines. Could there have been some sort of acrobatic entertainment provided by Abu Bakr II? The traveling Berber, Ibn Battuta, wrote that for a later Emperor in Mali: A group of young men "play and turn in the air as they do in Sind. They have a wonderful gracefulness and lightness in this...." Thomas Baker, artist, used computer technology to restore fragmentary prehistoric kiva paintings created centuries ago by the Pueblo Indians, which were discovered and excavated by the archaeology field school under Archeology Department Professor Frank C. Hibben of the University of New Mexico. (www.angelfire.com/grahamhancock.com based on Frank C. Hibben, *Kiva Art of the Anasazi at Pottery Mound*, KC Publications, Kiva 8, Layer 3, p. 118 fig. 89); compare with (right) Alseny Sylla or Sékou, "The Tumbling Beast from West Africa", 2017. Public domain.

Petroglyph of Camels on a Rock West of Los Lunas, New Mexico

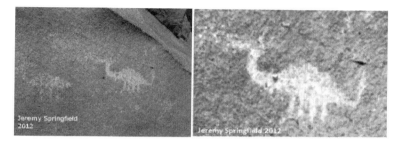

"The petroglyph above ... was discovered in 2012 by Jeremy Springfield on a trip to Hidden Mountain, just outside of Los Lunas, New Mexico. S8int website brought his story to our [Genesis Park's] attention. The drawing is located on an isolated, inaccessible ledge near a very clear deer petroglyph. What were the ancient Pueblo peoples intending to depict, if not a saurian creature that they knew from that region?" (from Genesis Park website) [Or do you think possibly it could be a Sahara Desert Camel?] Jeremy Springfield himself stated: "On a trip to Hidden Mountain, just outside of Los Lunas, New Mexico, on October 20th, 2012, I took pictures of what is possibly a dinosaur figure petroglyph. This is found on a mesa about 16 miles west of Los Lunas, and requires more than a mile's hike just to reach the foot of the mesa. The mesa contains scattered Native American art ... and ancient scattered ruins/ shelters on the summit. The attached photos were taken on the south-facing ridge of the mesa's summit, about 20 feet down from the ridge itself. The stone itself is quite protected from defacements and contemporary "tags" due to its difficult to reach location, which is only accessible by a perilous ledge some 14 inches wide that drops to a steep and deadly slope to the foothills some 400+ feet below." (from Aaron Judkins, PUEBLO PEOPLES ANCIENT DINOSAUR PETROGLYPH PHOTOGRAPHED IN NEW MEXICO? Posted by Chris Parker | Aug 27, 2013 "Pueblo Peoples Ancient Dinosaur Petroglyph Photographed in New Mexico?"; Posted: June 17, 2014 in Archaeology, websites) Pinterest, saved by Anna Oleksowicz. Photograph is in the public domain.

(top) A camel image from the *Catalan Atlas*, 1375, produced by the Majorcan cartographic school which is attributed to Cresques Abraham (also known as "Abraham Cresques"), a Jewish book illuminator, and (bottom) a boy astride a camel with tail raised (proving that camels do raise their tails to a vertical position as pictured in the Hidden Mountain petroglyph). Public domain.

Petroglyphs of Elephant and Camel on Rock near Suwanee, New Mexico

There is an interesting petroglyph of a Mali Empire elephant with a curving trunk (possibly as seen while carrying baggage), and a camel (dromedary) with a large hump and probable rider, found in the vicinity of the now abandoned Suwanee railroad stop (21 miles west of Albuquerque), New Mexico. Could this be the result of a prehistoric "show-and-tell"? How else could a prehistoric Native American make an extremely detailed petroglyph of two creatures that did not exist naturally in the North American Southwest, unless he or she witnessed them firsthand for himself or herself? Perhaps a Pueblo Indian from Zuni or Acoma witnessed the caravan traveling up the Rio Grande Valley, and on his way home was trying to explain what he had seen to some other Indian(s) by creating and "writing" this petroglyph. In this case, a picture is worth more than a mere thousand words. It almost tells the whole story of the African caravan all by itself!

Elephant with pack and camel with rider images adapted from Suwanee Petroglyph by Ronald Stewart. The cloven feet can be explained by the assumption that the original inscriber failed to see the elephant's feet in the tall grass of the valley.

A fully loaded elephant which explains why the Suwanee Petroglyph probably has what appears to be a hump. Unknown drawing adapted by Ronald Stewart.

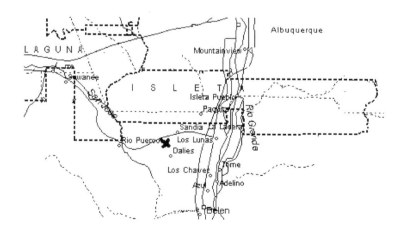

Map of New Mexico USA - Los Lunas Hidden Mountain [camel] marked by an **X**; Suwanee [elephant+camel] on left under" N" in LAGUNA. Map adapted from an unknown map maker's map by Ronald Stewart.

"The petroglyphs were made primarily by using a stone or two stones like a hammer and a chisel to gently peck off the patina on the boulder's surface and creating the image the artist desired to create. Images started being created like this around the year 1300 and became known as the "Rio Grande Style"[48] The meaning of petroglyph images is in the eye of the beholder, as well as in the mind of the original Indian engraver. Our interpretation of them varies with our past experiences, knowledge of Indian culture, and of course, our active imagination. Some would call it pareidolia.

Indian creating a petroglyph or pictograph in 1924, based on photograph by Edward S. Curtis. Photograph is in the public domain.

Possible Petroglyph of an Elephant in Albuquerque, New Mexico

Dr. D. Clark Wernecke, warns in an article titled "It is good to be reminded that our eyes can easily pick out what we want to see [pareidolia] and that many claims should be checked and rechecked".[49]

A case in point occurred to the author while searching for evidence of elephantid petroglyphs on the west side of the Rio Grande where part of the city of Albuquerque now stands. Pueblo Indians have pictured New Mexican fauna on these black basaltic rocks for centuries. The native artists knew well the anatomy of such local animals as lizards, snakes, birds, rabbits, coyotes, sheep, deer, etc.

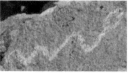

Lizard/snake/bird photographs from Petroglyph National Monument. Public domain.

But their knowledge of the African elephant's anatomy would have been incomplete due to the caravan's short visit in the future Albuquerque region of villages like Alameda, Isleta, Piedras Marcadas (marked stones) and many others.

There is this curious animal petroglyph in Petroglyph National Monument's Boca Negra Canyon (with three critical features—tail, ears and snout sloughed off—or could it have been intentionally chiseled off because it was not thought by someone that pre-historic Indians of the Rio Grande Valley could possibly have seen elephants like this?):

Compare this elephant with hidden feet with an unknown quadruped petroglyph with critically missing features (sloughed off or chiseled off) at Boca Negra Canyon, Petroglyph National Monument, Albuquerque, New Mexico. (Note the possible angular breathline in the lower right corner identifying it as made by a Pueblo Indian). Upper photograph by US Fish & Wildlife Service from FreeStockPhotos.Biz. Lower photo of possible elephant petroglyph courtesy of Joanne Stewart, May 23, 2016.

Remember, these talented artists were inscribing animal features on rocks from memory, not from sketches or by large animals modeling for them in the rocks. Therefore, the artists may not have remembered exactly what the feet or ears looked like. It would have been the trunk that they would have found fascinating. What were the nearby Indians trying to communicate with these fantastic images—local quadrupeds, or passing elephants? If they were elephants, could they have been Mali's Sahara Desert elephants, known for their large foot pads, longer legs and smaller body mass, or could they have been the bush elephants known as the largest and heaviest land animals, or perhaps they were even forest elephants from the Congo Basin. Could they have even been a mixture of these types, each with their own special talents for imperial transportation, fighting capabilities or baggage carrying? The rocks are silent on that subject.

A sign in this Boca Negra Canyon states that: "Most petroglyph images in the park are dated by relative dating techniques. The design elements are compared to dated pottery and prehistoric Puebloan murals. The murals had colorful painted images on the plaster walls of kivas (subterranean ceremonial rooms). Many of the mural images are not found before 1300, which suggest that new ideas were beginning to emerge in Pueblo culture." One has to wonder if Abu Bakr II's caravan of foreign knowledge and culture had something to do with these emerging ideas. Was there an impact by the Emperor's people on Native American peoples? The rocks are silent.

Celebrating End of the Drought: Kuaua Black Figure Thought to be Responsible for Bringing Rain.

Rio Grande, bosque (grove of trees) and Sandia Mountain. Photograph courtesy of Joanne Stewart, July 18, 2018.

The 35 mile long Sandia Mountain to the east of the Rio Grande, east of the Emperor's path up the valley, was sacred to the earliest inhabitants of the region. To some of them it was known as *Oku Pin* or South World Mountain, the dwelling place of *Oku'wapin* who watches over the valley. Even today it is considered by some as a special place of reverence. Did the Emperor experience the sun's haunting glow at dawn as light slowly peeped over the crest? Did he marvel at the colorful and amazing watermelon (Spanish *sandia*) tint of the western escarpment at sunset? Did he quake in fear at the reverberating sounds of thunder coming from the water laden, menacing clouds above the mountain top situated over 10,000 feet above sea level? Or did he hide from the mountain's monsoon rains beneath his hand held umbrella (see image) as the Kuaua Pueblo's painted Kiva portrait suggests? Perhaps, or he might have relished the sudden appearance of moisture, as the Native Americans must have, after so many days and months of drought.

Photograph courtesy of Joanne Stewart, July 18, 2018

It must have been the beginning of the annual monsoon rainy season (late June or early July) when Abu Bakr II's caravan approached Kuaua (Evergreen) Pueblo, along the west bank of the Rio Grande just north of the present site of Bernalillo, New Mexico, and facing Sandia Mountain to the east. One can imagine that as Abu Bakr II approached Kuaua Pueblo, the sky above the Rio Grande opened up and the monsoon rains finally began to fall after a prolonged drought. "Several notable droughts extended across much of western North America, including severe and sustained droughts in the ... medieval period, between 900–1300.... These droughts appear to have exceeded the duration and magnitude of any subsequent droughts in western North America."[50] Droughts had serious consequences for peoples of the North American Southwest, causing famine and relocations from agriculturally marginal farms, dried up streambeds, isolated cliff dwellings and desert homes to better watered sites such as those in the Rio Grande Valley.

This painted mural figure in Kuaua Pueblo's *kiva* #3 (Museum of New Mexico's Coronado State Monument [now Coronado Historic Site] near Bernalillo, Sandoval County, New Mexico) has been variously identified as a Pueblo priest in a rain-making ceremony, or a clown—but could it really have been honoring the goatee [white "V" on painting] wearing Mali Emperor with his "imperial umbrella" (right hand) and "Commander-in-Chief bow" and "rain pot" (left hand) for supposedly bringing rain to the Rio Grande Valley? Some Pueblo Indian traditions associated pots with rain gods (usually held in a hand). Tesuque Pueblo potters still produce rain god figurines with pots for the tourist market. Finally, could the white framing curve on the left represent an elephant's ivory tusk, just like the imperial elephant's tusk that probably framed the Emperor when he stood in front of his ponderous beast? This author believes that it does.

Lydia Chinana, embroiderer of Jemez Pueblo, described storm designed embroidery, which may explain the background of the Kuaua Kiva painting this way: "The [black] thunder is always in the middle, and then you have

71

steps on the side, and the rain. Those are always the same, you can't change." However, murals were sometimes enhanced with streaks of yellow lightning, utility storage jars, and other meaningful symbols explaining pictorially what the people could not express in written form. This author believes that the black figure is just such a symbol-filled picture providing the viewer with all sorts of information about the visiting Emperor of Mali.

Reproduced by Ronald Stewart

Image created by Dr. Ronald Stewart, based on his work as first Coordinator of New Mexico State Monuments, 1970-1972.

Umbrellas, as seen in the right hand of the kiva figure, were noted by Antonio de Espejo's party in 1582 in one of the Rio Grande Pueblos. "We saw umbrellas like Chinese parasols, painted with the sun, the moon and the stars", his chronicler observed.[50] This chronicler, Diego Pérez de Luxán, covered the journey with a manuscript titled *Relación de la expedición de Antonio de Espejo a Nuevo México, 1582-1583* (*Expedition into New Mexico made by Antonio de Espejo 1582-1583*).

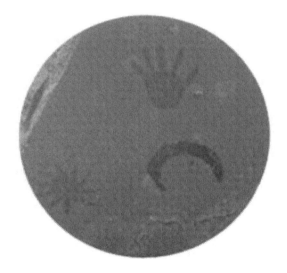

Moon, star, etc. (possibly crab nebula supernova) pictograph in Penasco Blanco, Chaco Culture National Historical Park, New Mexico. Photograph is in the public domain.

Could the umbrella sighting have been at Kuaua? Possibly, since it is said that " … umbrellas are banned at [present-day] Pueblo feast day dances because it is considered a sin to prevent life-giving rain from falling all the way to the ground." (From "Coronado Historic Site's Black Drops of Rain", New Mexico Museums & Historic Sites, summer guide 2015, page15). Perhaps it was Kuaua Pueblo's people that were the "umbrella exception"—due to umbrella using Abu Bakr's entourage's probable willingness to trade their rain and sun protecting umbrellas for food.

Reconstructed underground Painted Kiva (ceremonial chamber, men's club) at Kuaua Pueblo during monsoon season. "For them (Pueblo Indians), summer is the season of 'male rain'—a season of short, intense afternoon rainstorms accompanied by plenty of thunder and lightning." (From "Coronado Historic Site's Black Drops of Rain", New Mexico Museums & Historic Sites, Summer Guide 2015, page15). Photograph courtesy of Joanne Stewart, July 18, 2018

Dr. Marc Simmons, noted New Mexico historian, has analized painted kiva images like this: "Dr. Bertha Dutton who in 1963 wrote the story of their recovery stated that Kuaua's murals are 'clear portrayals of folk history.' They are, indeed. And much more!"[52, 108] In this case, a picture truly is worth a thousand words, and reminds the author of a saying: "Reading is for people who don't understand pictures!" One could read about how this rain associated figure is one thing or another, but not until you actually see it do you understand its full significance as an indicator of a visitor from Africa who became a "rain maker" for one Pueblo Indian artist.

The Kuaua Indians probably welcomed their new "rain spirit" with jubilation and religious fervor. They undoubtedly believed this strange visitor, with his strange, mysterious, gigantic beasts, had divinely created this miracle of moisture—so long desired after decades of drought. They probably wondered how best to properly honor him, when their best artist stepped forward and suggested that he be allowed to paint another figure on the wall of the sacred underground kiva. But did Abu Bakr II stay around Kuaua long enough to witness his divination ceremony and finished portrait? Possibly, but he was also anxious to continue his quest westward, so as soon as he could leave without offending the adoring Pueblo people, he probably did.

Since turquoise pendants have been unearthed at Kuaua Pueblo ruin, it is almost certain that Abu Bakr's people would have acquired, through trade, pieces with drilled holes through them for personal adornment. Or would they have looked down their noses at these semi-precious stones the way some Indian peoples did at gold that later the Spanish found so desirable?

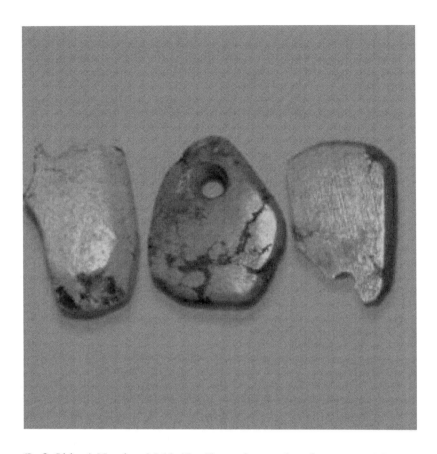

(Left Object) Number 36.12.47—Turquoise pendant fragment—1.5 cm x
1.0 cm. roughly rectangular, fragment of pendant broken through
perforation width and lengthwise, chalky green. (Center Object) Number
36.12.48—Turquoise pendant—1.8 cm x 1.5 cm. Flat irregularly shaped
pendant perforated at smaller end, green with rust matrix. (Right Object)
Number 36.12.49—Turquoise pendant fragment—1.4 cm x 1.0 cm.
nearly rectangular flat broken pendant, broken across corner through
perforation, light green. From Coronado Historic Site, Artifact of the
Week, 6-4-14, posted by Ethan Ortega. Public domain.

Ahfitche, called Jose Quivera, Governor of San Felipe Pueblo, demonstrating the pump and drill method of making holes in turquoise and shells. Public domain photograph taken by John K. Hillers at San Felipe Pueblo, New Mexico in the winter of 1880.

The Emperor's caravan probably next encountered the Eastern Keres speaking pueblo people at Katishtya, aka San Felipe, where hundreds of men, women and children, dress in traditional Green Corn Dance costume and dance throughout the day, accompanied by a male chorus.

Corn Dance at San Felipe Pueblo, New Mexico, photo from Library of Congress. Photograph is in the public domain.

Utility jars, like the following, could have been used to hold rainwater, cornmeal and other food products. The Emperor's party possibly utilized jars like that when they traded for food and drinking water.

Katishtya (San Felipe) storage jar, Courtesy of The Amerind Foundation, Inc., Dragoon, Arizona,   Catalog No. 5756. Photograph by Eric J. Kaldahl. Public domain.

Probably next on the Emperor's list of "must see" sights, according to his scouts, would have been the Kasha-Katuwe or Tent Rocks near Cochiti Pueblo. The Bureau of Land Management states that:

> The cone-shaped tent rock formations are the products of volcanic eruptions that occurred 6 to 7 million years ago and left pumice, ash, and tuff deposits over 1,000 feet thick. Tremendous explosions from the Jemez volcanic field spewed pyroclasts (rock fragments), while searing hot gases blasted down slopes in an incandescent avalanche called a "pyroclastic flow".

Precariously perched on many of the tapering hoodoos are boulder caps that protect the softer pumice and tuff below. Some tents have lost their hard, resistant caprocks, and are disintegrating. While fairly uniform in shape, the tent rock formations vary in height from a few feet up to 90 feet."

Kasha-Katuwe or Tent Rocks (now a National Monument) near Cochiti Pueblo, New Mexico, are cone shaped volcanic pumice, ash and tuff formations. Photograph courtesy of Joanne Stewart, July 16, 2018.

Black "Chakwaina" Kachina

An interesting "*kachina*" exists in Keresan, Zuni and Hopi Pueblo cultures that may have had its inspiration in the person of the Emperor. "It has been said that the *kachina* known as *Chakwaina* (*Tsakwayna*) represents Esteban the Moor, who led Fray Marcos de Niza in search of Cibola and was killed at Zuni. [However,] Barton Wright, a noted Katsina expert said this is not likely because the *kachina* *Chakwaina* originally came from the Rio Grande pueblos, migrated to Zuni, then to Hopi from Zuni."[53] This *kachina,* according to Robert Goodwin's *Crossing the Continent, 1527-1540,* may actually predate contact with the Spanish.

Apparently Chakwaina was based on a warrior of great renown, brandishing a bow, bandolier of cowrie shells, buckskin kilt and sometimes a golden skull-cap. "Although imagery of the *kachina* is varied, it is usually depicted as an ogre, with ferocious [white] teeth [bright red lips] and a black goatee and [or] black mask with yellow eyes."[54] This latter *kachina* is known as "the nephew". (Did Abu Bakr II bring his nephew along with him?) Sometimes, the "Chief of Warriors" or "long beard" *kachina* has bulging black eyes encircled with white bands (the idea of protruding eyes will come up again when a Navajo myth is discussed). This one is known as "the uncle". The buckskin skirt supposedly indicates that he was a hunter too. Did the Emperor join his Indian hosts on a deer, elk or antelope hunt—or could it have been a dangerous buffalo hunt from the back of an elephant?

(left) "*Chakwaina Kachina*" or "*Tsa'kwynakatsina*" image of Abu Bakr II with thick lips, white teeth and sporting chin whiskers (goatee like Kuaua Kiva painting). He wears a double cowrie shell bandolier, golden *usekh* (Egyptian style broad collar), golden skullcap (crown), golden armbands and golden bracelets (all indicating his wealth). In his hands he holds a golden bow showing that he is Commander-in-Chief of his army and marines, and a crook (scepter?) as an emblem of his Imperial Authority (or a rattle that *Chakwaina* dancers use, or is it an umbrella?). (*Kachina* sculpted by Ronald Stewart based on various pictures of Indian *Chakwaina kachinas*; photograph courtesy of Alicia Stanton). (right) Bulging eyed "masque de Kachina CHAKWAINA MANA, HOPI, Arizona" for a dancer by Piotr Tarnman on ArtStation, https://www.artstation.com/artwork/vK3B3. not copyrighted.

Does the *kachina*'s bulging eyes indicate that Abu Bakr II suffered from protruding eyes, (technically called proptosis)? This protruding eyes indicator in the *kachina* is supported by a Navajo creation myth.

(top) Golden Pectoral of Ip Shemou Abi, King of Byblos (Phoenicia). Beirut National Museum, O.Mustafin (Own work). From Wikimedia Commons. Public domain.

The *kachina* also sports a version of the Royal Egyptian and Middle Eastern *Usekh*, pectoral or golden broad collar. The royal collars were connected with clasps of gold. Since Esteban never reached the Rio Grande pueblos, *Chakwaina* must have been based on some other great leader of black warriors—could it be umbrella holding (as pictured in Kuaua Kiva), bow wielding, *usekh* (golden broad collar) wearing, golden skull-capped Abu Bakr II (as pictured earlier)? If so, then the Emperor did not travel casually. He maintained his imperial persona and authority by wearing the *usekh*, his golden cap (crown), and golden bracelets, as well as holding onto his bow probably symbolizing his authority as commander-in-chief. One *Chakwaina Kachina* has a shell bandolier. Cowrie shell bandoliers were the prerogative of kings and priests in West Africa.[55] Since it is pictured on *Chakwaina*, the Emperor actually may have worn a bandolier of cowrie shells (especially *Monetaria moneta*), which were used for centuries as a currency in Africa. Ibn Battuta described how, in Gao: "The buying and selling of its inhabitants is done with cowrie-shells, and the same is the case at Niani" (Abu Bakr II's Mali capital). Did Abu Bakr II use cowrie shells for trading purposes in the Southwest, or was it just for displaying his wealth and imperial status? Did he have a goatee or chin whiskers because he was also imitating Egyptian Pharaohs and their false chin beard? After all, Egyptian royalty probably had been the sole role model for isolated Mali royalty.

(left) "Bulgy Eyes" (head). Bronze. H: 26.2 cm. Found in Benin City, Yoruba Culture. Image courtesy of George Ortiz Collection. Public domain. It is said that "bulging eyes represent an extreme of the Oshugbo convention suggesting spiritual force and presence," and mystical strength, from Bruno Claessens; (right) Yoruba agere ifa (divination cup]) featuring a talking drum player. Note bulging eyes. Height: 18.5 cm. Collected by Leo Frobenius in 1912. Image courtesy of the Ethnologisches Museum (SMPK), Berlin, Germany (III C 27097). Public domain.

The Diné (Navajo), some of whom may have arrived in northern New Mexico by 1312, had this to say in their First World (Ni'hodilhil) Creation Story: ***"came a whole crowd of beings. Dark colored they were, with thick lips and dark, protruding eyes."***[56] It may be impossible to positively link these mythical creatures (black ant people) with the Emperor and his long ant-like line of caravan people descending Cañon Largo, nevertheless, it is an interesting point to ponder and speculate about. Is it impossible due to time difference? Maybe, but "Scientists, believe that some Athapaskan bands [later called Apache and Navajo by the Spanish] first came to the American Southwest around the year 1300."[57] The timing would appear to be right.

Aniceto Swaso, of Santa Clara Pueblo, stated that:

> Through song the Katsina [Kachina] teaches the Indian people how to live correctly: "Children, you must mind your parents or the earth will crack and the wild man will come out and eat you. You must not drink water while you are eating or all your teeth will fall out. When your first teeth fall out in the daytime do not throw them away in the daytime, but wait until evening and then ask your grandmother for new teeth. When you are cooking, wash your pot when you take it from the fire, so that its lips will not get sore. And take the stone that you set the pot on outdoors so that it won't sweat all the time. Little girls, if you play with little boys you will never grow tall, but you will always be short. And if the little boys go with the girls,

they will never grow up at all." Aniceto also said: "I know these things are true, because this is what I have heard from my grandmother, Hemokyatsik.[58]

One can just imagine the grandmother storytellers' tales about *Chakwaina* (Abu Bakr II). Storytellers became a major inspiration for pueblo potters like J. Lucero.

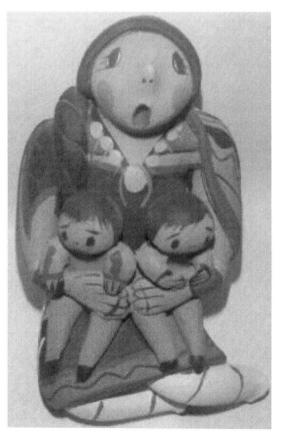

Ceramic "Storyteller" by J Lucero, Jemez Pueblo, New Mexico. Photograph is courtesy of Joanne Stewart (own pottery collection).

Another famous version of *Chakwaina* (Abu Bakr II):

President John F. Kennedy was presented with a Long Beard (*Chakwaina*) *Kachina* [now thought by this author to be an image of Abu Bakr II] from the Two Graces Gift Shop in Taos, New Mexico, in the early 1960's. He gave it to his daughter Caroline where it became part of the Caroline Kennedy Doll Collection in the John F. Kennedy Presidential Library & Museum. (left) KN-27018 (right) photograph by Heather Joines Mason, Museum Specialist. Photographs courtesy of the John F. Kennedy Presidential Library & Museum.

Did *Chakwaina Kachina* become a device to teach children to beware of strangers, or was it an Indian "boogie-man" designed to scare children? A Hopi individual informed the author that the *kachina* known as *Chakwaina* was used to keep children from going out and wandering away at night. As an example, he told the author that when he was young and sleeping in a kiva with the men of the clan, *"Chakwaina"* was supposedly heard making noise and walking across the roof. What better way to convince the children that there was danger from wolves, coyotes, bears, mountain lions and ogres outside at night! Some Pueblo people considered *Chakwaina* to be "the Great Hunter" and "the Chief of Warriors".

Other Rio Grande pueblos that the Emperor couldn't help but encounter were Kewa, also known as Santo Domingo, site of the *"Sandaro"*, which is a burlesque with lots of clowning; and Ko-tyit, also known as Cochiti, where drums were made from hollowed out logs and easily traded because of their excellent quality and tone.

Linen postcard showing Pueblo Indians making hollow log drums, circa 1930-1945, created/published by Alfred Mc Garr Adv. Ser., Albuquerque, N. M., from The Tichnor Brothers Collection, Boston Public Library, Print Department. No known restrictions.

Since the Emperor was probably a keen explorer, he would have taken side trips to see as much as he could. His scouts would have led him into the Galisteo Basin to visit more pueblos. Ya'atze, also known as San Marcos (Spanish name), may have been nearly a hundred years old when the Emperor saw it near the Galisteo River. He would have marveled at the extensive agricultural landscape around the Pueblo which included pebble-mulch fields, rock-bordered gardens, borrow pits, terraces, and check dams. The village would have appeared to have been a significant manufacturing center for the ceramic types included in the Rio Grande glaze wares. This pottery was exported in large quantities from this pueblo to other pueblos in the upper Rio Grande area and possibly as far away as the southern Plains. The Emperor could have traded at this Pueblo for food, pottery, lead and turquoise from nearby mines. The pueblo of Ya'atze, or San Marcos, was one of the largest prehistoric pueblos in the United States, with approximately 2,000 ground-floor rooms. It was approximately 2½ miles east of Mt. Chalchihuitl. It may, from its beginnings around 1300 to its abandonment during the Pueblo Revolt of 1680, have controlled, to some extent, the turquoise and lead mines of the Cerrillos Hills. Today, Cerrillos Hills State Park, located off the Turquoise Trail National Scenic Byway between Santa Fe and Albuquerque, "is dedicated to the creation, enhancement & stewardship of the historical, recreational & cultural open space in the Cerrillos Hills, Santa Fe County, New Mexico, USA". This includes hiking and equestrian rides through the historic turquoise mining district, but there isn't any mention of elephant or camel riding in the park's literature. What a shame!

There is an abundance of turquoise debitage (waste flakes) at San Marcos, indicating quantities of turquoise were processed there, but not a great number of finished turquoise pieces. Turquoise was traded in all directions. Hernan De Soto's 1540's Spanish expedition to the Mississippi Valley from Florida was even told that the turquoise came from the West. Mt. Chalchihuitl turquoise was highly valued by Indian tribes all over the Southwest and it is assumed that the Pueblo of San Marcos benefited from its location close to the mines. An analysis of potsherds found at the O'Neil Blue Bell turquoise pits to the south of Mt. Chalchihuitl has determined that 75% of them came from San Marcos Pueblo, and that 95% of them date from 1300s through the 1600s.

The Keresan settlements are as follows, those marked with an asterisk being extinct: Acoma (west of Albuquerque), Acomita (west of Albuquerque), Cieneguilla (Tziguma)*, Cochiti, on the Rio Grande, north of Santo Domingo (Kewa), Cubero*, Cueva Pintada*, Gipuy*, Haatze*, Hasatch, Heashkowa*, Huashpatzena*, Kakanatzatia*, Kashkachuti*, Katzinio*, Kohasaya*, Kowina*, Kuapa*, Kuehtya*, Laguna (west of Albuquerque), Moquino*, Paguate, Pueblito, Puerto (?)*, Punvekia, Punyeestye, Pusityitcho, Rito*, San Felipe (on the Rio Grande, north of Santa Ana), Santa Ana (Tamaya) (on the Rio Grande, north of Bernalillo), Santo Domingo (Kewa) (on the Rio Grande, north of San Felipe), Seemunah, Shumasitscha*, Sia (Zia), Siama, Tapitsiama*, Tipoti*, Wapuchuseamma, Washpashuka* and Yapashi*

The following pueblos, now extinct, perhaps were also Keresan: Alipoti, Ayqui, Cebolleta, Pelchiu Pueblo del Encierro, San Mateo, Tashkatze, and Tojagua. Adapted from https://www.accessgenealogy.com/native/keresan-pueblo-indians.htm.

Los Cerrillos, New Mexico, Mining District—Cerro del Oso from the
Saddle of Archíbigui (H. Milford Collection, no. 90). Public domain.

Los Cerrillos, New Mexico, Mining District, the old Chachuitl turquoise mine looking east, photographed about 1883 by William H. Brown (H. Milford Collection, no. 93) Public domain.

William P. Blake, the first geologist to visit Mount Chalchihuitl, described it in Journal XII, in the entry of August 29, 1857. The following is Blake's journal entry for Mt. Chalchihuitl:

> A great chasm or excavation, basin shaped, with projecting crags and precipices. 200 feet deep—300 wide—an enormous excavation into the solid rock and a pile of debris equally enormous. Trees growing in the bottom and at the sides, 20 feet high pines & very old. The

rocks have caved in. A cave or shelter cut into the crags where Indians even now lodge.

Leaving the arroyo we ascended the slope of the hill following a foot trail among the cedars & gradually ascending until we reached the brink of a precipice which stopped our progress. Here we dismounted and clambering down among the crags looked off into an enormous basin shaped excavation below in the bottom and along the sides of which pine trees were growing. This excavation is nearly circular and is bounded on three sides by vertical precipices of rock, rugged and supporting trees here and there in the crevices.
.

I was so much struck with the extent of this singular excavation that it was some minutes before I could believe that it was the work of men alone and for an ornamental stone whatever it might prove to be. I looked in vain for traces of a mineral vein or bed of ore which might have attracted miners but there were none. In extent this opening is not less than 300 feet in length and breadth and 200 feet deep and it must have been made the greater part of it centuries ago. The immense heaps or debris of the rock which has been removed is strewn out on one side and forms quite a hill which is over covered with pines —sufficient evidence of the antiquity of the opening. This is not the only pile of rocks which have been removed they are found on all sides and in most places are covered with lichens, gray with age. All the rock appears to have been broken up into fragments not larger than the fist or of eggs and then carried out and turned over the bank of refuses.

The great opening is surrounded by several of less magnitude but—yet—quite extensive and the result of much hard labor. That such an extensive excavation and breaking away of the hard rocks can be the work of Indians without powder seems incredible but such it undoubtedly is. It cannot have been worked for any of the metals and the evidence presented at the locality is sufficient to show that it was not made in pursuit of either gold or silver but that it was made solely to procure the chal chee wee te. Looking carefully among the debris I found small fragments of the blue stone which I was assured is the much prized chal-chee-wee-te it resembled Turquoise which a subsequent careful examination found it to be. It occurs only in thin seams or veins traversing the solid rock and I should judge that it is rarely over ¾ of an inch in thickness. Several masses of the old debris remained long ago show the mineral in blue spots and thin scales on the surface but specimens freshly broken out have a greenish color and are different from that of the turquoise in common use in jewelry. It is probable that specimens are seldom over the thickness mentioned but some fragments nearly half an inch in diameter may have been obtained.

Indians through the centuries developed methods of mining and working turquoise that produced all sorts of jewelry and pieces of religious importance. Artifacts found by archeologists include chicken ladders (notched poles) for entering mine shafts, grooved stone mauls and antler picks plus quartz tipped bow drills and other handheld tools for creating finished pieces. The Emperor of Mali undoubtedly would have been impressed with the whole turquoise mining, working and trading process since he personally had owned the gold mines of the Mali Empire.

The Galisteo Basin was a treasure trove of Tano or Tewa speaking peoples practicing irrigated agriculture, hunting pronghorn antelope and bison, and trading with Plains peoples as well as the Rio Grande Valley peoples.*

Unless the whole caravan traveled up the Galisteo River Valley and turned northward at San Marcos Pueblo proceeding up over the hills and back to the Rio Grande River, the Emperor's caravan would have encountered a steep wall of rock blocking its way—La Bajada (Spanish for "The Descent").

"La Bajada, or 'the descent,' marks the division between the Rio Arriba, or 'upper river,' and the Rio Abajo, or 'lower river,' sections of New Mexico. This steep and dangerous grade was long an obstacle to caravan traffic going from the Rio Grande Valley to Santa Fe." Photograph courtesy of Joanne Stewart.

La Bajada's escarpment near Cochiti Pueblo, New Mexico, July 13, 2018, photograph courtesy of Joanne Stewart

La Bajada's 600 foot escarpment has been a major obstacle for travelers ascending or descending the Rio Grande Valley ever since the lava flow abruptly halted, forming a basaltic cliff littered with huge blocks of black rock and a talus slope of smaller debris. However La Bajada provided good quality basalt for lithic tools and a mixture of useful plants and animals for the nearby inhabitants such as those at Cochiti and its outlying small pueblos. The Emperor may have been overawed by La Bajada's rugged scenic qualities, but probably also full of dread at the prospect of taking elephants up its steep and treacherous side.

The Emperor's caravan of elephants, camels and possibly other quadrupeds, such as horses and donkeys, probably followed an Indian trail along the Santa Fe River in the Cañon de Las Bocas from Santo Domingo Pueblo, through the yawning canyon of Las Bocas (the mouths) and up Cienega Creek, over to Cieneguilla and north up the Rio Grande. The shortest route over La Bajada escarpment was the trail through Cañon de Las Bocas or the mouth of the

Santa Fe River, southeast of the La Bajada escarpment. The alternatives were to head eastward through the gentler slopes of the Galisteo Basin and Cerrillos Hills, or attempt to scale the 600 foot escarpment—an almost impossible task.

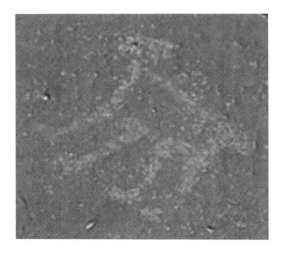

An Indian petroglyph of an unknown animal on a La Bajada rock. Was it supposed to be a mythical creature, a clan totem, a native New Mexican four legged hunting symbol—or could it have been one of the Emperor's caravan quadrupeds? This photograph is in the public domain.

---

* Following is a list of Tano or Southern Tewa pueblos so far as known:

Cienega, Colina Verde (on San Cristobal Ranch), Dyapige, Galisteo or Ximena, Guika, Kayepu, Kipana, Kuakaa, Ojana, Paako (east side of Sandia Mountain), Pueblo Blanco, Pueblo Colorado (on San Cristobal Ranch), Pueblo de los Silos, Pueblo Largo (on San Cristobal Ranch), Pueblo Quemado (on the Santa Fe River), Puerto(?), San Cristóbal, San Lázaro, San Marcos, Sempoapi, Shé (on San Cristobal Ranch), Tuerto, Tungge, Tzemantuo, Tzenatay and Uapige. Adapted from https://www.accessgenealogy.com/native/tano-pueblo-indians.htm.

The Santa Fe River tree line below La Bajada Hill, near Las Bocas, New Mexico, July 13, 2018, photograph courtesy of Joanne Stewart

The poor condition of the Santa Fe River trail was lamented by Diego De Vargas. In an excerpt from his diary he describes the difficulties he faced at the Cañon de Las Bocas:

> *"The entire force was gathered in readiness at about five o'clock in the afternoon, at which time I sallied forth from the pueblo* (Santo Domingo) *with the said camp. After traveling less than a league, we found the ... slope so rough and washed away, due to continuous rains and a long period of disuse, that it was necessary to reopen the way, and by hand and the strength of strong arms we pulled through. ... For this reason I encamped at a place called Las Bocas. The entire camp arrived after dusk. And since the road was so rough and difficult, we were obliged to spend the night on the plain which surrounds the ridge or mountain there."* Diego De Vargas—1692

As the caravan of elephants, camels and Africans continued its way up the Rio Grande valley, up and over (or possibly around) the basaltic La Bajada escarpment, they crossed the La Bajada Mesa toward the Rio Arriba (Spanish for "Upper River"). These river hills are called the Cerros del Rio because the Rio Grande cuts through their western flank, boxed in between the hills and the Jemez Mountains. In fact the more common name for this area is the Caja del Rio, (Spanish for "River Box"). Located between the two volcanic fields of the Caja del Rio and the Jemez Mountains, the Rio Grande has carved the wide White Rock Canyon, rimmed by dark basalt.

Rio Grande at White Rock Canyon; From Northern New Mexico Loop: part 1- Santa Fe to the Jemez by blisterfree. Public domain photograph

On his way, the Emperor may have encountered even more Tewa speaking pueblos and small communities in the Santa Fe River Valley and at La Cienega. The Emperor would have been greeted with *Be-pu-wa-ve*, "Welcome" since his eagerness to trade instead of attacking would have been well known by then.

Northern Tewa towns and villages still occupied: Tesuque (8 miles north of Santa Fe), Nambe (about 18 miles north of Santa Fe, on Nambe River, a small tributary of the Rio Grande), San Ildefonso (near the eastern bank of the Rio Grande, about 23 miles northwest of Santa Fe), Ohkay Owingeh (or San Juan near the eastern bank of the Rio Grande 25 miles northwest of Santa Fe), and Santa Clara (on the western bank of the Rio Grande, about 25 miles above Santa Fe).*

---

*Towns and villages formerly occupied by the Northern Tewa:
Abechiu (at a place called Le Puente, on a bluff close to the southern bank of Rio Chama, 3 miles southeast of the present town of Abiquiu, Rio Arriba County), Agawano (in the mountains about 7 miles east of the Rio Grande, on Rio Santa Cruz), Analco (at the place where there is now the so-called "oldest house," adjacent to San Miguel Chapel, in Santa Fe), Axol (location uncertain), Camitria (in Rio Arriba County), Chipiinuinge (on a small but high detached mesa between the Canones and Polvadera Creek, 4 miles south of Chama and about 14 miles southwest of Abiquiu, Rio Arriba County), Chipiwi (location uncertain), Chupadero (location uncertain), Cuyamunque (on Tesuque Creek, between Tesuque and Pojoaque, about 15 miles northwest of Santa Fe), Fejiu (at the site of the present Abiquiu on the Rio Chama, Rio Arriba County), Fesere (on a mesa west or south of the Rio Chama, near Abiquiu, Rio Arriba County), Homayo (on the west bank of Rio Ojo Caliente, a small western tributary of the Rio Grande, in Rio Arriba County), Howiri (at the Rito Colorado, about 10 miles west of the Hot Springs, near Abiquiu, Rio Arriba County), Ihamba (on the south side of Pojoaque River, between Pojoaque and San Ildefonso Pueblos), Jacona (a short distance west of Nambe, on the south side of Pojoaque River, Santa Fe County), Junetre (in Rio Arriba County), Kaayu (in the vicinity of the "Santuario" in the mountains about 7 miles east of the Rio Grande, on Rio Santa Cruz, Santa Fe County), Keguayo (in the vicinity of the Chupaderos, a cluster of springs in a mountain gorge, about 4 miles east of Nambe Pueblo), Kuapooge (with Analco occupying the site of Santa Fe), Kwengyauinge (on a conical hill about 15 feet high, overlooking Chama River, at a point

101

known as La Puenta, about 3 miles below Abiquiu, Rio Arriba County), Luceros (partially Tewa), Navahu (in the second valley south of the great pueblo and cliff village of Puye, west of Santa Clara Pueblo, in the Pajarito Park), Navawi (between the Rito de los Frijoles and Santa Clara Canyon, southwest of San Ildefonso), Otowi (on a mesa about 5 miles west of the point where the Rio Grande enters White Rock Canyon, between the Rite de los Frijoles and Santa Clara Canyon, in the northeastern corner of Sandoval County), Perage (a few rods from the west bank of the Rio Grande, about 1 mile west of San Ildefonso Pueblo), Pininicangui (on a knoll in a valley about 2 miles south of Puye and 3 miles south of Santa Clara Creek, on the Pajarito Plateau, Sandoval County), Pojiuuingge (at La Joya, about 10 miles north of San Juan Pueblo), Pojoaque, on a small eastern tributary of the Rio Grande, about 18 miles north-west of Santa Fe), Ponyinumbu (near the Mexican settlement of Santa Cruz, in the northern part of Santa Fe County), Ponyipakuen (near Ojo Caliente and El Rito, about the boundary of Taos and Rio Arriba Counties), Poseuingge (at the Rito Colorado, about 10 miles west of the hot springs near Abiquiu), Potzuye (on a mesa west of the Rio Grande in northern New Mexico, between San Ildefonso Pueblo on the north and the Rito de los Frijoles on the south), Pueblito (opposite San Juan Pueblo, on the west bank of the Rio Grande in Rio Arriba County), Pueblo Quemado (or Tano) (6 miles southwest of Santa Fe), Puye (on a mesa about 10 miles west of the Rio Grande and a mile south of Santa Clara Canyon, near the intersection of the boundaries of Rio Arriba, Sandoval, and Santa Fe Counties), Sajiuwingge (at La Joya, about 10 miles north of San Juan Pueblo, Rio Arriba County), Sakeyu (on a mesa west of the Rio Grande in northern New Mexico, between San Ildefonso Pueblo and Rito de los Frijoles), Sandia (not the Tiwa pueblo of that name), Santa Cruz (east of the Rio Grande, 30 miles northwest of Santa Fe, at the site of the present town of that name), Sepawi (in the valley of El Rito Creek, on the heights above the Ojo Caliente of Joseph, and 5 miles from the Mexican settlement of El Rito), Shufina (on a castle-like mesa of tufa northwest of Puye and separated from it by Santa Clara Canyon), Teeuinge (on top of the mesa on the south side of Rio Chama, about . 4 mile from the river and an equal distance below the mouth of Rio Oso, in Rio Arriba County. Tejeuingge Ouiping (on the southern slope of the hills on which stands the present pueblo of San Juan, on the Rio Grande), Tobhipangge (8 miles northeast of the present Nambe

Pueblo), Triapf (location uncertain), Triaque (location uncertain), Troomaxiaquino (in Rio Arriba County), Tsankawi (on a lofty mesa between the Rito de los Frijoles on the south and Los Alamos Canyon on the north, about 5 miles west of the Rio Grande), Tsawarii (at or near the present hamlet of La Puebla, or Pueblito, a few miles above the town of Santa Cruz, in southeastern Rio Arriba County), Tseweige (location uncertain), Tshirege (on the northern edge of the Mesa del Pajarito about 6 miles west of the Rio Grande and 7 miles south of San Ildefonso Pueblo) and Yugeuingge (on the west bank of the Rio Grande, opposite the present pueblo of San Juan, near the site of the village of Chamita).
The following extinct villages are either Tewa or Tano:
Chiuma (location uncertain), Guia (on the Rio Grande in the vicinity of Albuquerque), Guika (on the Rio Grande near Albuquerque) and Peas Negras (on an eminence west of Pecos Road, near the edge of a forest, eight miles south-southeast of Santa Fe). (Adapted from https://www. accessgenealogy.com/native/tewa-pueblo-indians.htm)

North of present day Santa Fe, the Emperor undoubtedly would have been brought by his scouts to a rocky hill near the Tesuque Indian Pueblo. Here was a sight not to be missed. Was it an ominous omen that indicated that he should have brought more camels instead of elephants on this journey?

Camel Rock, Tesuque Pueblo, New Mexico, July 13, 2018, photograph courtesy of Joanne Stewart

It would have been a nostalgic moment for the Emperor's party for there before them sat a huge camel made of rocks —a single humped camel similar to the ones he brought with him and those loaded with gold and salt that traversed the Sahara Desert between Mali and Mediterranean Sea.

Camels with a howdah, by Émile Rouergue, 1855, from Wikipedia, "Camel train". This image is in the public domain.

Tesuque (Te Tesugeh Oweengeh, meaning the "village of the narrow place of the cottonwood trees.") was the next Tewa speaking pueblo that the Emperor's caravan would have entered after viewing "Camel Rock". It is just north of present-day Santa Fe.

The roofs and ovens of Tesuque Pueblo, New Mexico, Bennett, G. C.—
Photographer—from Robert N. Dennis collection of stereoscopic views. /
United States. / States / New Mexico. / Stereoscopic views of the Indians
of New Mexico. This image is available from the New York Public
Library's Digital Library under the digital ID
G90F462_040ZF: digitalgallery.nypl.org → digitalcollections.nypl.org.
This half of a stereoscopic photograph is in the Public Domain.

The next pueblo might have been Nambé-O-Ween-Ge
("People of the Round Earth") whose residents performed
dances and other ceremonies above Nambé Pueblo at the
spectacular Nambé Falls. But did they perform for the
Emperor?

Nambe Falls, Nambe Pueblo, New Mexico, author: <u>kenkopal</u>, 16 May 2008, 09:28:32. Licensed under the Creative Commons Attribution-Share Alike 2.0 Generic license. Wikimedia Commons. Public domain.

106

Near the future site of Española, south of Taos, the Emperor was forced to make a crucial decision—to enter a deep, narrow gorge farther up the Rio Grande Valley that obviously limited the amount of grass growing there, or chance the rim where he would have been told that little fodder for elephants grew.

View of the "Rio Grande—Wild and Scenic River" from Wikimedia Commons. The Pueblo peoples also had names for the Spanish named Rio Grande/Rio Bravo: Keresan, *mets'ichi chena*, "Big River"; Tewa, *posoge*, "Big River"; Tiwa, *paslápaane*, "Big River"; Towa, *hañapakwa*, "Great Waters". Public domain.

To make matters worse, the horizon would have revealed to his scouts that steep, snow clad mountains lay ahead—mountains that it would be cruel to force elephants to traverse. After all, a mountain was just a mountain, and if it did not contain the minerals he sought, and the prospectors possibly claimed it didn't, then, he would have had no interest in it, especially if it wasn't in the direction he wished to travel—West.

Rocky Mountains, July 13, 2018, photograph courtesy of Joanne Stewart

Probably the Emperor's original intention was to travel westward to find the next shore, or his African home. So he likely took his caravan of explorers up the northwestward valley of the Rio Chama. The Chama Valley would have been the first westward trending valley of an adequate size for finding animal fodder of which the Emperor would have approved. It would also have served the purpose of getting the Emperor a few miles closer to his starting point in Mali.

Posi-ouinge or *Posi*, the 'Greenness Pueblo', near Ojo Caliente (hot spring or "where warm waters halt" according to Tewa legend and the Forrest Fenn treasure poem) was just one of ten or more pueblos that utilized the waters of the Valley and its tributaries like Rio Ojo Caliente. After enjoying the warm waters of Ojo Caliente springs that Abu Bakr II's Indian guide or scouts probably pointed out to him, the rested expedition would have continued to a point where

108

the valley narrowed, so the Emperor would have instructed his men to take as much river and spring water as the elephants could carry, climb out of the Chama Valley (perhaps up the Puerco River Valley) and through the dry country until they found another lush valley. If he was lucky, helpful Pueblo Indians from Tewa speaking *Posi-ouinge*, or another pueblo near Abiquiú, anxious to rid themselves of this large food consuming army, would have guided the Emperor's party along a long established trading and migrating route through the dry uplands, across the 7,300 foot Continental Divide and downward through *cañones*, like Cañon Largo, into the San Juan River Valley (an old Tewa Indian of Santa Clara Pueblo, Aniceto Swaso, declared some years ago that his ancestors in ancient times had migrated down from Mesa Verde in Colorado, passing along the banks of the Chama, and pausing briefly at the site of Abiquiú, before continuing on to the Rio Grande).

It is said that: "Archaeologists know at least ten significant pueblo sites along the Chama River, between present day Abiquiú and Rio Grande. Modern Abiquiú is probably located on the site of an abandoned Indian pueblo, but about three miles east of the site of the present town on the point of a gravel-capped terrace 100 to 150 feet above the level of the Chama River on the south side lie the extensive ruins of the pueblo of Po-shu-ouinge, which was abandoned prior to the Spanish occupation. The pottery found in the excavation of this ruin included a wide variety of pre-Spanish types—and the association is believed to be explained by a tradition of the Pueblo Indians of Santa Clara and San Juan that Po-shu-ouinge was a place where fairs were held and where many people came to trade and to have a fiesta.[59] The valley was a major trade route between the San Juan River area and the Rio Grande Valley."[60]

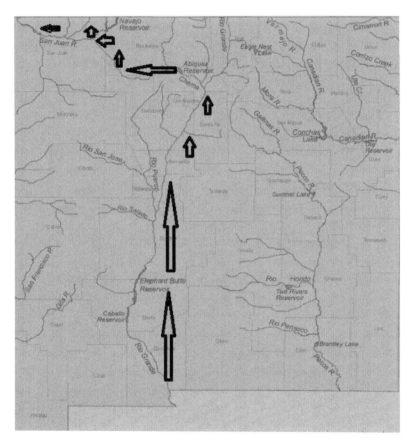

New Mexico map showing the Native American migration/trading trail and 1829 Antonio Armijo Route of the Old Spanish Trail between Chama River and San Juan River. This is a Public Domain map with arrows indicating direction of Emperor Abu Bakr II's route northward and westward added by Ronald Stewart.

The route that the Emperor's caravan took between the Chama and San Juan Rivers is unknown, but could have been up one of the Pueblo Indian migrating or trading routes to the San Juan Valley, such as the Spanish fathers Fray Francisco Atanasio Domínguez and Fray Silvestre Vélez de Escalante followed, in part, approximately 464 years later in 1776. Their description probably differed little from the Emperor's route over the Continental Divide, and thus might suffice for purposes of this discovery.

Dominguez and Escalante made the following observations:

> ... we set forth from the pueblo of Santa Rosa de Abiquiu toward the west along the bed of the Chama River and traveled in it a little less than two leagues. We then turned northwest, and having gone about three and a half leagues over a bad road [trail?], for in it there are some small and very stony mesas, we halted for siesta on the north side of the valley of La Piedra Alumbre [The Alum Rock], near Arroyo Seco [Dry Gulch]. They say that on some mesas to the east and northeast of this valley alum rock and transparent gypsum are found. In the afternoon we set out from Arroyo Seco toward the north. After going a short distance we turned northeast along a wooded canyon and having traveled two leagues over a very bad road [trail?] we camped on the banks of the same arroyo. (South of Canjilon) Today a good shower fell upon us, and we traveled seven leagues [a

111

league equaled the distance that could be walked in one hour—farther on level ground than on hilly terrain].

We set forth up the same canyon toward the northeast. After going a little more than four leagues we turned north, and entered a wooded canyon ..., the same stream which lower down they call Arroyo del Canjilon, or Arroyo Seco. Having passed through the grove, we came to a small plain of abundant pasturage which is very pleasing to the sight, because it produces some flowers whose color is between purple and white .... Where these flowers begin the canyon is divided into two by a high mesa which enters it. In each branch there is a road [trail?], one of which runs north and the other west. At the beginning of the latter and under the southern point of the mesa there is a little spring of good permanent water.... We continued our march by the western canyon and road [trail?] and traveled a league and a quarter to the north. Then, after going less than half a league to the west, we turned northwest, and having traveled a little more than three leagues over good terrain we arrived at a small stream called Rio de la Cebolla .... From here we went forward in the afternoon, turning north about a quarter of a league to get back to the road [trail?] which we had left. We swung northwest, and having traveled a little more than three leagues over

112

good terrain we halted in a small plain on the bank of another arroyo, (near Cebolla on Nutrias Creek) which is called Rio de las Nutrias. Today eight leagues.

We went northwest from Arroyo de las Nutrias [beavers], entered a small grove of pines, and having traveled a little less than three leagues we descended to the Rio de Chama. Then, along its pretty meadow we went up to the north about a mile, crossed it.... The meadow of the river is about a league long from north to south, and is of good land for crops with opportunities for irrigation. It produces much flax and good and abundant pasturage, and there are also the other advantages necessary for the founding and maintenance of a settlement. Here also there is a good grove of white cottonwoods. In the afternoon we went forward, and after climbing the western bank of the river we entered a small valley which we called Santo Domingo. Three large mesas covered with pines, beginning with three small hills almost north of here, curve around it from north to south to form a semi-circle reaching to the river. They (the companions who had been here previously) told us that to the west of these mesas there are two lakes. The first and more southerly one is west of the pass which from this bank can be seen between the first and second mesas, and the second is to the west of the next opening, which likewise can be seen between the second and the third mesas. These lakes, as well as the valley, are very suitable for raising large and small stock. We continued through the valley toward the northwest and entered a small grove of pines.... We had to camp on rough ground near the three small hills already mentioned and which we named the Santisima Trinidad, (about five miles northwest of Park View) having traveled from the river only two leagues to the northwest. In this place there was no permanent water, although we found a little in an arroyo near the broken ground to the east-southeast.... Today five leagues.

Setting out toward the north from the camp of Santisima Trinidad, we traveled two leagues through the same forest ... Two large mesas surround it, each forming a semi-circle, the north end of one almost meeting the south end of the other, the two being separated by a narrow gateway or pass. We traveled about a quarter of a league to the northwest and went through the pass where begins another lake which we called Laguna de Olivares. It must be about a' quarter of a league long and two hundred varas [*vara* = 33 inches] wide, more or less. Although its water has not a very pleasant taste it is fit to drink. From the lake and little pass we continued north half a league, then turned northeast, leaving the road which goes to the Piedra Parada (Standing Rock, still so-called) (a place known to those of us who have traveled through here). The guides directed us through a chamise thicket without any trail or path whatsoever, saying that on the road we were now leaving there were three very bad hills, and that it was less direct than the route they were taking. We traveled a little more than a league and in the same chamise thicket again turned west-northwest, entered the forest (which continues), and after half a league swung northwest. We then traveled three and a half leagues through a valley with very luxuriant pasturage and came to a large meadow of the arroyo which on the Piedra Parado road they call Arroyo del Belduque [large knife] In the meadow we swung west and having traveled down the arroyo two leagues we camped in a canyon [near Dulce] which, on account of a certain incident, we called Canon del Engano [deceit]. Today nine and a quarter leagues. Here there is plentiful pasturage and water in pools.

We set out from camp in the Canon del Engano toward the southwest and having traveled half a league arrived at Rio de Navajo, which rises in the Sierra de la Grulla [San Juan Mountains] and runs from northeast to southwest to this point, where it turns back toward the north for a little more than three leagues, and then joins another river which they call the San Juan. Here this Navajo River has less water than the Chama.

Painting of Dominguez and Escalante in the Utah State Capitol from https://americangallery.wordpress.com/2012/08/16/lee-greene-richards-1878-1950/

Having crossed the river we continued with difficulty toward the south in the same canyon, and after going about a league we turned to the southwest for a quarter of a league, then three quarters of a league to the west through canyons, over hills, and through very difficult brush. The guides lost the trail and even seemed to have forgotten the very slight knowledge which they had appeared to have to this country. And so, in order not to go any farther south we turned northwest, traveled about three leagues without a trail, climbing a hill, high but with no very difficult grade, and saw the bed of the same river nearby. We descended to it down slopes which were somewhat rugged but nevertheless passable, and having traveled a little more than three leagues westnorthwest, we crossed it at a good ford and camped on the north bank. Here it has already united with the San Juan River. The guides told us that a little higher up these two rivers joined, so we decided to observe the latitude of this campsite and for this observation was made by the meridian of the sun, and we found the campsite, which we named Nuestra Senora de las Nieves, to be in latitude 37°51' [camp was on the San Juan River near Carracas, just across the Colorado state line]. Fray Silvestre went to examine the place where the two rivers, the Navajo and the San Juan, join and found it was three leagues as the crow flies almost due east of Las Nieves (the snows), and that on the banks of both rivers, right at the junction, there were good advantages for a fair-sized settlement. The San Juan River carries more water than the Navajo, and they say that farther north it has good and large meadows because it runs through more open country. Now joined, the two streams form a river as large as the Rio del Norte in the month of July.... Today eight leagues.

In the afternoon we left the camp of Nuestra Senora de las Nieves, going downstream toward the west, and having traveled two and one-half leagues over bad terrain, we camped on the bank of the river [about four miles east of Arboles (trees)]. Today two leagues and a half.

We continued a little more than a league to the west along the bank of the river and on the slopes of the adjacent mesas, climbed a somewhat difficult hill, swung northwest, and after going one more league arrived at another river which they call Rio de la Piedra Parada ,... This river rises to the north of the San Juan in the same Sierra de la Grulla (crane), runs from north to south, and is a little smaller than the Chama River where it passes through the pueblo of Abiquiu.[61]

Too bad the Emperor didn't have this road sign to tell him when he was over the continental "hump". Photograph courtesy of Joanne Stewart

Rio Puerco near New Mexico State Route 96, showing abundant vegetation. Photograph courtesy of Joanne Stewart, June 18, 2017

There is another more probable route—the 1829 Antonio Armijo mule train route westward taking advantage of creeks, meadows and arroyos (normally dry watercourses)

like Rio Puerco, Poleo Creek, Agua Sarca, Salitral Creek, Arroyo Jaspe, Cañon Pinabetoso, Rito del Ojo, Rio Capulin, Rio Gallina, Salt Draw, Cañada Jacquez and Cañon Largo, with springs on both sides of the Continental Divide.

Cañon Largo, New Mexico near US Route 550, showing sufficient vegetation for grazing animals. Photograph by R. Stewart June 18, 2017.

Whichever way the Emperor was guided, whether it was along the northern route of Dominquez and Escalante or the 1829 southern route of Antonio Armijo's 60 man, 100 mule caravan up creeks, arroyos, canyons and valleys and down Cañon Largo, the journey over the Continental Divide would not have been an easy one. Elephants are said to be able to travel about four days without water. However, the approximately eight day Armijo route (or some other Indian trail) was probably at times a dry, difficult and dreary scene. At the very least it would have been challenging for man and beast. In addition, there were lots of elk, mule deer, coyotes, wolves, bobcats, tarantulas, black bears and grizzly bears , mountain lions , and rattle snakes to be seen—or felt. Here also resided the ancestors of the Navajo or Diné. "The first Navajo land was called Dine'tah. Three rivers—the San Juan, the Gobernador, and the Largo ran through Dine'tah, which was situated just east of Farmington, New Mexico"[62]

On the dry and dreary Pacific side of the Continental Divide: "Cuervo Canyon at junction of Canon Largo, [near] Blanco, San Juan County, NM", public domain photograph from the Library of Congress.

Cibolo Canyon Elephant Petroglyph

Clay Johnston, Site Steward for Northwest New Mexico, reported seeing an elephant petroglyph in Cibolo Canyon, a tributary of Cañon Largo, according to Larry Baker, Executive Director of the San Juan County Archeological Research Center and Library at Salmon Ruins (this author was its first Director in 1973). Did a Navajo person etch a member of this strange caravan in stone for show-and-tell purposes?

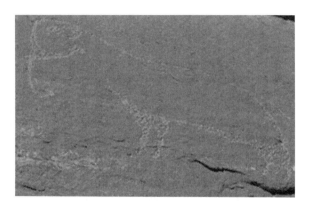

Elephantlike petroglyph in Cibolo Canyon near Cañon Largo indicating that perhaps Abu Bakr II's caravan did pass westward through Cañon Largo. Photograph by Bob Young of Farmington, New Mexico; used with his permission on July 16, 2018. Bob Young believes that "This particular canyon contains images primarily Navajo in origin with some Puebloan P3-4 images and occasional Basketmaker images. There are no Archaic or earlier images. This is a quadruped with a short tail, an apparent trunk, the suggestion of a tusk and small floppy ears. The head is in line with the back. This certainly resembles a young elephant, possibly Indian. The lack of significant patina in the pecked areas would indicate an image of about 150-250 years. There were traveling circuses in the 1800s or the artist may have seen such an animal elsewhere."

Did some of the Diné (Navajo), when they encountered the single file, ant-like procession, just watch them ramble down the arroyo toward the San Juan River Valley, noting their appearance in the Black World Creation Myth as the Wo'ia'zhini Dine'è or "Black Ant People" thusly: *"After these* [coyotes, wasps and spider ant people] *came a whole crowd of beings. Dark colored they were, with thick lips and dark, protruding eyes. They were the black ants.... and after the different ant people ... there came others...."*[56] Did the Diné trade with them? Did they learn anything from them? The myth is silent about these possibilities. Perhaps the myth about "others" is referring to the elephants and camels for which the Diné had no words, or possibly to the lighter-skinned Tuareg and/or Berber camel drivers from the Sahara Desert that probably accompanied the Emperor. It may be impossible to positively link these mythical creatures with the Emperor and his long ant-like line of caravan people descending Cañon Largo, nevertheless, it is an interesting point to ponder and speculate about. Is it impossible due to time difference? Maybe, but "Scientists, believe that some Athapaskan bands [later called Apache and Navajo by the Spanish] first came to the American Southwest around the year 1300."[57] The timing would appear to be right. Some of today's ruins like Tapacito, Split Rock, Hooded Fireplace, Largo School and Crow Canyon near Cañon Largo, although defensive in appearance, could date to an earlier era. Since the Diné (Navajo) people are credited with adopting, agricultural and equine techniques from the Pueblo Indians and Spanish, one wonders if they also could have learned some other useful things from these intrepid African adventurers.

"Elephant Slabs" of Flora Vista, New Mexico—Proof of Mandinka Writing Visitors from the Mali Empire in Africa

Finally, Emperor Abu Bakr's thirsty caravan reached the San Juan and Animas Rivers where the elephants could bathe to their heart's content and drink (elephants can drink two hundred liters or fifty three gallons of water per day). What a relief that must have been!

Elephants crossing the Luangwa River, South Luangwa NP, Zambia. Attribution: (WT-en) Jpatokal at English Wikivoyage, Wikimedia Commons, Creative Commons Attribution-Share Alike 3.0 Unported license.

At this point, one has to ask what concrete evidence and proof exists for this caravan reaching the San Juan and Animas River Valleys. The answer is two Flora Vista "Elephant Slab" stone tablet inscriptions.

Clyde Winters Ph. D. expressed this belief in the forward of Dr. David Imhotep's book: "In the American Southwest.... the most interesting Malian artifacts from the Southwest are the Elephant Slabs. These remains, which came to the Arizona State Museum in 1950, were found buried in a pueblo ruin room on the south bank of the Animas River near Flora Vista, New Mexico. This Malian inscription depicts elephants and birds on the tablets in addition to Mande symbols.... These inscriptions" stated Dr. Winters, "were written by the followers of Abubakari the Great, a ruler of the ancient Mali Empire who made an expedition to the Americas in early 1300's. Members of the Mali expedition left numerous inscriptions throughout the New World. Evidence shows that they wrote in the Manding writing system, which is understood by using the (African) Vai script to read the Mande inscriptions the Malians left in the Americas. I [Dr. Clyde Winters] deciphered the Malian inscriptions in 1977."[63]

David Henige, in Project Muse's "Inscriptions Are Texts Too" stated that "... the contents of inscriptions, whatever else, are texts trying to tell some kind of story.... Epigraphic evidence is a virtual *terra incognita* for Africanists; few of our sources have come down to us from the past quite so directly", speaking of epigraphs in Gao, Mali, but equally applicable to the Flora Vista inscriptions. Between May 9, 2007–August 26, 2007, The Smithsonian's National Museum of African Art in Washington, D.C., featured an exhibit titled *Inscribing Meaning: Writing and Graphic Systems in African Art*. This exhibit "recognized that "Africa's long engagement with written and graphic systems is part of the broader, global history of writing and literacy."

125

Two slabs of rock known as "the elephant slabs" recorded the passage of the Mali elephants at a small pueblo near Flora Vista, New Mexico, which was located on a tributary of the San Juan River known as the Animas River. Paul F. Reed, of the Center for Desert Archaeology, has written that: "During this time [1100s-late 1200's], the Puebloans of the Totah [a Navajo Word for 'between rivers' meaning between the San Juan and Animas Rivers] emerged as a political entity, with regional centers at Salmon [Ruins, site of San Juan County Archeological Research Center and Library] , Jacquez, and the Point site on the San Juan River; Aztec Ruins [National Monument], the Blancett site, and the Flora Vista site on the Animas River;..."[64]

The (privately owned) Flora Vista, New Mexico, pueblo ruin site on June 18, 2017. One of several photographs of the site taken by Joanne Stewart.

What the boy who found the "elephant slabs" might have thought: *Wouldn't it be great for a 10 year old like me to live in a Pueblo with lots of other children? I would eat wild asparagus, corn, beans, squash, venison and turkey—and maybe even swim in the nearby Animas River with the cute elephants pictured on my stone elephant slab.* Collage by Ronald Stewart.

Ninety three year old Harold S. Gladwin, in a letter to Dr. Barry Fell of The Epigraphic Society stated that:

> During the summer of 1929, I and several other members of the staff of Gila Pueblo [Archeological Foundation], including Ted and Monroe Amsden, were conducting an archaeological survey on the Mesa Verde National Park in the southwestern corner of Colorado. In August, Mr. A. M. Amsden, father of the Amsden boys, came up from Farmington, northwestern New Mexico, to visit us and see what we were doing, He was very enthusiastic and when he learned that the construction of Gila Pueblo had actually begun, he said that he had something that which he valued very highly but which he intended to give to the Pueblo. In due course he returned to our camp and presented a small stone tablet to me which shows several rows of figures which he regarded as hieroglyphs of some unknown language.

> The tablet is 5 ¾" x 6" in size and not more than ¼" in thickness. The colour is chocolate brown, the same as the earth in which it had been found, but a small chip off the right top corner shows that the slab itself is sandstone of a rather yellowish colour. The surface, including the incised figures, is covered with

what appears to be a deep patina or desert varnish.

Original Flora Vista, New Mexico "Elephant Slab #1" with its upper right corner in place—before being lost. Attributed to (now dissolved) Gila Pueblo Archeological Foundation in Arizona prior to 1950.

A corrected version of the "sketched markings" (as Dr. Clyde Winters calls them) of "elephant slab #1" which was once erroneously identified as "Anasazi tablet with mammoth" (from dinosandhumans.org.). In actuality, this one-of-a-kind rectangular "elephant slab" (with zone of inundation symbol on restored upper right corner in this author's version) is probably an eye-witness account of a prehistoric flood in northwestern New Mexico, with river bend (Animas River?), sunrise, sunset, lightning and storm symbols, but most importantly with seven flooded land, and two stone hut (pueblo) symbols as well as outlines of two elephants and two birds. Corrected by Ronald Stewart.

After thanking Mr. Amsden, I asked him to tell me as much as possible about the history of the tablet. He told me that a young boy had come into his office of his bank in Farmington, about twenty years ago, and had shown him the tablet with the chip missing from the right top corner. He wanted to sell it for one dollar. Mr. Amsden gave him a dollar and added that he would give him another dollar if the boy could show him exactly where it had been found and could find the missing chip.

The boy took Mr. Amsden to a small [stone] ruin on the south side of the Animas River opposite the small settlement of Flora Vista, a few miles above [northeast] of Farmington. He pointed to a small area of disturbed earth in a room, outlined by rock walls, where he had been digging with a trowel. Mr. Amsden knelt down and turned over the loose dirt and, surprisingly, found the chip which was noticeable because of the yellow colour of the fresh break. Digging a little deeper, they found a second tablet, 14 ½" x 7 ¾", triangular, with a single row of hieroglyphs, which was later given to Dr. Earl H. Morris, of the University of Colorado at Boulder. The finding of the chip and the second tablet were convincing evidence that the boy had told the truth as to the exact location where the first tablet had been found.

In 1950, the first tablet was given to the Arizona State Museum at the University of Arizona in Tucson, and in 1953, Dr. Morris presented the second, triangular, slab to the Museum with the statement: 'Whatever these slabs may be, they should be kept together. <u>I believe them to be authentic and hope that sooner or later something will turn up to reveal their significance'</u> [underlining by this book's author].

[Ronald Stewart's note: Flora Vista Tablet (rectangular "Elephant Slab") (14.6 cm x 15.6 cm x .95 cm) as seen by the author and photographed by Joanne Stewart—without the lost corner chip—in the Arizona State Museum Curator of Collections office on May 13, 2015]

In 1964, Mr. E[Edwin] B[ooth] Sayles, now in Tucson, but formerly on the staff at Gila Pueblo, took the tablets to the Arizona Bureau of Mines and later received a report that the tablets were:

'A limey sandstone, source unknown, showed nothing under ultra-violet, no fluorescence. High magnification examination shows that designs were retraced. Method of retracing unknown, but quartz, chalcedony, or obsidian would have been adequate.'...

The most to hope is that the inscriptions on the tablets may, someday, tell their own story. [underlining by book's author]

[signed] Harold S. Gladwin
Santa Barbara
June 12th 1975"[64]

Dr. Dennis L. Swift stated that: "Earl H. Morris, a noted authority on south-western Indian artifacts [mentioned in the above letter], says the Flora Vista ruins date at about ad 1200, so the ancient artist could not have seen his elephant in a circus, zoo or a book. An excavated mammoth skeleton would not show that it had a trunk, so the artist obviously saw a live elephantid of some sort still alive in the region only hundreds of years ago."[66]

In an excerpt of a letter of Mr. Gladwin dated 8-11-52, which appears in the catalog records of the Arizona State Museum, Gladwin stated that:

> In due course, Earl Morris heard about the slab and did some digging of his own. Earl succeeded in finding another slab—the long triangular piece which also had an elephant inscribed on it. Unfortunately, Earl tried to improve on the original with the point of a nail and wound up with some raw scratches that might have been made last week.

A statement by Earl Morris, dated 4-2-1953, found in the Arizona State Museum, refuted the above assertion, saying:

> In regard to the two inscribed stone slabs, one in the possession of the University of Arizona Museum [Arizona State Museum] [#52822] and the other in my own collection [Arizona State Museum #A-11946], I will make the following statement which in some respects will differ from that made by Mr. Gladwin in his letter of 8-11-1952.
>
> These two slabs were found in a ruin on the south side of the Animas River opposite the little settlement of Flora Vista. Mr. A. M. Amsden purchased both slabs from a boy who lived at Flora Vista. The boy took Mr. Amsden to the spot where he had found them and later Mr. Amsden took me back to the same place. Through his son, Charles, Mr.

Amsden gave the smaller [rectangular] more complete slab to the Southwest Museum [Arizona State Museum] and later on he gave me the larger irregular one from which the cast [#52823] now in the University of Arizona Museum [Arizona State Museum] was made.

Mr. Galdwin's statement that I did some digging at the spot and found the larger slab is not so. Nor neither is it true, as he puts it, '

"Earl tried to improve on the original with the point of a nail and wound up with som (sic) raw scratches that might have been made last week." I have in no way tried to improve or retouch the original.

I can see no reason to doubt the authenticity of these specimens, [author's underlining] but how to explain them I would not know. In all of my experience I have seen nothing similar. They presumably date rather late because most of the potsherds on the ruin where they are supposed to have been found are of Mesa Verde wares.

Mr. Gladwin's statement that the stones came into Mr. Amsden's possession in the 1920's is somewhat in error. I do not remember the exact year but I am certain that it was previous to 1910."

SEE: Acces. Perm. – Earl Morris
for additional information.

Mr. Gladwin continued, stating:

"In 1929, when we were surveying in Mesa Verde, Mr. Amsden came up and presented the small square slab to Gila Pueblo. For a number of years the slab and its broken corner were in our Stone Room, but I am sorry to say that the corner fragment eventually disappeared as a result of Joe's cleaning operations. When Earl heard that we had the Amsden [rectangular] slab, he sent us down his own triangular slab and Pete Havens made the plaster cast which you now have. Unfortunately, Pete must have been careless in packing Earl's slab, when it was returned to him, as I understand that it was broken into two pieces in transit.

You will have to use your own judgment as to the significance of these two slabs from Flora Vista. Most of the archaeologists who saw them at Gila Pueblo condemned them immediately as fakes. Harry Mera thought that they might be Mormon tablets which someone had buried with the idea of staging a "revelation". Personally [stated Gladwin], I am a sucker for things of this kind and am inclined to believe that they are genuine [author's underlining] until they can be proved to have been fakes. There is certainly nothing in the appearance of the square [rectangular] slab that gives me any reason to think that they were faked. Particularly since there is no doubt that they were actually buried and dug up in the ruin at Flora Vista.

Arizona State Museum catalog #A-11946: "Found at same site as #52822. Roughly triangular in shape. On one face, close to the edge of one of the long sides [top], are the pictographs [petroglyphs]---a procession of animals and other objects. One looks like a long-legged bird, another like an elephant, and another is a quadruped with a long tail." The one line irregular "elephant slab" possibly translates right to left as *a dog (or some other unfortunate quadruped) was struck by lightning (quadruped + struck by + lightning) [☁✝🐾] which scared the "residue" (shit?) out of the elephant [🐘⬛] and caused the bird(s) to fly away across the inundated land [🦅🍴✦]*.

"Elephant Slab #2" photo courtesy of Joanne Stewart, May 13, 2015

There has been keen interest in the "elephant slabs" in the past, but no one has satisfactorily explained their existence. For example, critic Jason Colavito has stated that: "I think that one look at the drawing should strongly imply that the slabs are forgeries made by someone with only a passing knowledge of ancient alphabets. The symbols are nonsense and do not conform to any known written language" and "If they truly represented a European or African language, surely the same characters should be in use in the Old World" [author's note: they were, they were on rocks in the Sahara

137

Desert and on tree bark]. Jason Colavito continued: "For now, there is no reason to doubt the scientific consensus that these are fake stone tablets created by unknown persons for an unspecified purpose."[67] [This was not a widely known written language—only the elite "secret society" of nobles, priests, merchants and certain blacksmiths knew of its use].

A humorous but curious attempt at translation by someone named Dixie Perkins appeared in a book by Debora L. Carr titled *You Don't Need a Passport To Move to New Mexico— A Transplanted Easterner's Humorous View of Life in New Mexico,* Indianapolis: Dog Ear Publishing, 2009, p. 117.

First slab: *"To leave with the bird, this animal to arrive alive with the haughty cat"*

Second slab: *"Tame the bird in the house to ward off agitation. Raise the elephant to perish. To build a dome and be free of the elephant. Direct the hand and follow to grasp the neck band, piercing to make an opening to affect the heart. Hoard to bear a dome for cover to overcome misery on a journey with goods for sickness. Give attention to. Use."* (After some examination she announced that the symbols must have been ancient *Iberian* … circa 400-100 BC.)

 On the other hand, Barry Fell (former president of The Epigraphic Society) after studying the inscriptions for ten years, thought that the tablet script must have come from Indonesia or the Caroline Islands of Woleai, Ifaluk, Faraulep or Eurapik, and were possibly "magical talismans"[68]

Barry Fell's translations of tablets:

A talisman reliable, this is powerful magic. This is a Javanese talisman, reliable, of merit, full, powerful (for your) wishes secret. The pictopraphs [sic] avoid E erasure. The script preserve, to enable a person to avert always danger.

However, Dr. Clyde Winters is of the opinion that "The inscriptions [erroneously deciphered by Perkins and Fell] relate to the Malian expedition to the Americas..."[69] and he (Dr. Clyde Winters) provided the following transliteration/decipherment of the first slab on the web site "Ancient Origins" on July 24, 2016:

Ga gya Birds [image] Kpa nde ngbe Ka go ne
Sama (elephant) [image] ga ka bi kpa
Ni ngbe nde kai Sama [image] gya Sun [image] (ga kpa)
Pe kpe gbe nge gya
De kpa ne mbe nde bi-nu gya
Gya pe ndɛgyi ngba kai ga
Gyi nde pɛ du ke nu
Ga gyi Sun [image]

Life (is spent) removing thou sick elephants dried up by the sun. Many are sick. (The dead elephants) are pushed down (into a hole/buried) and sealed on the flat terrain adjoining the bed of the river (at) the dry place-- the zone of inundation. My existence at the present family habitation is lean. (On) dry land adjoining the bed of the river break up the terrain for cultivation (and) thou cut the hearth. Break to pieces the flatlands to carve and make the family habitation. Warmth, water, Sun [image].

Dr. Winters also has provided the following possible transliteration and translation of "Elephant Slab #2":

Dè ki bird [image] gba Sama (elephant) [image] bo-kpo gbe-kpe ka-kpo dè be Bear [image].—Uncultivated land, hunt the birds, cook the elephant (it is) easy to roast, grow on the flat terrain the maize (in) arid uncultivated land. There are also bears.[70]

There are certain errors in the "sketched markings" which may not have been taken into account by Dr. Winters, or other translators. First, the "sketched markings" indicate that these markings were made sometime after the upper right corner of the first or "A" slab was found missing. A magnified view of that missing chip (which can be seen in the original photograph of the stone slab) indicates that several symbols, one of which resembling a trident (one of seven on the first slab) which Dr. Winters translates as "land of inundation" or "zone of inundation"[71], have been truncated. Secondly, several others symbols on the first slab were erroneously copied into the "sketched markings". Thirdly, the second slab's last image of a long tailed quadruped has been variously interpreted as a dog, cat, mountain lion or bear. Obviously, it cannot be all of them. The original stone inscription contains longer quadruped legs than those indicated in the "sketched markings" In other words, one should not count on the "sketched markings" when interpreting the inscriptions, but should use the original photograph of the first slab and peruse the actual elephant slabs themselves, which are in the Arizona State Museum collection.

This author believes that the "elephant slabs" are authentic due to their similarity to an Arizona cave inscription, and are West African, related to the documented historic exploration by Mali Emperor Abu Bakr II about 1312 CE. The importance of these two prehistoric inscribed stones should not be overlooked, or belittled, by historians of the Southwest. Rightly or wrongly, this author strongly believes that they are the key to African exploration of the American West during the early 14th century, as well as an eye-witness account of a natural phenomenon—a FLOOD.

Dr. Clyde Winters described the history of the scripts of Mali this way:

> ... due to the demands of trade, scripts were invented by African trader groups in ancient times. This was especially true of the Mande or Manding-speaking peoples who are recognized as the inventors of several scripts. It appears from the evidence that these writing systems were not recent creations. They were derived from a proto-Mande script invented thousands of years ago by the ancestors of the Mande when they lived in the Sahara at the time it was fertile. This proto-Mande script was used by the ancient Mande to write or

141

engrave inscriptions throughout the Western Sahara.[71]

K. Hau has stated that "The ancient Mande wrote on stone, wood and dried palm leaves"[72] The term *guy mbind* or "Baobabs of writing" was a common phrase in West Africa. "Though the secrets of these trees are now lost, and the priests and the nobles [the so-called "secret society"] of olden days are now gone, local people still treat these trees with great respect."[73]

There are examples of West African writing on Sahara Desert rocks, tree trunks and written documents like this:

An example from the largest corpus of documents written in African scripts that exists in sub-Saharan Africa, located in the Bamum Palace, Foumban, Cameroon (US Embassy Yaoundé) Public domain.
http://photos.state.gov/libraries/475/08a06/080406-AfricanScripts-500.jpg.

After a journey across the parched continental divide, one of the restricted "secret society" of writers (probably a member of the Emperor's court, noble, priest, merchant or blacksmith) of the Mali Empire wrote a "newspaper-like" article (with follow-up). This author believes that perhaps in addition to Dr. Winters' decipherment of some of the elephants' demise (due, no doubt, to the dry and hot conditions of crossing the continental divide), there is more to the tale. Could the seven flood symbols on the first elephant slab indicate an eye-witness account of a prehistoric lightning storm resulting in an Animas River flood—written in stone? The animal figures and storm symbols are so realistic that they may have been inscribed by someone who had sculpting or engraving experience.

This author has developed his own additional interpretation of the Flora Vista Elephant Slabs based on Sahara Desert and West African symbols found on the internet. A total of seven symbols of "Y" for "zone of inundation" and three in boxes of [symbol] for "water"[74] are seen on the stone, indicating that it was a serious flooding event that the engraver was reporting. One possible translation might go something like this: The land is inundated. The stone hut (pueblo) is flooded. The numerous birds [symbol] are doing something near the flooded stone hut [symbol] at a bend in the river [symbol] and the elephants [symbol] are doing something at sunrise [symbol] near the flooded stone hut(s) [symbol], (also known as pueblos). But, the real story here may be that the valley land is being inundated by a flood aggravated by lightning storms (read right to left) [symbol] [a symbol for inundation +

143

water/rain symbol with a right side "lightning" diagonal]. At sunset [𝕣] there was even more rain [▨].

Picture of the May 23, 2005, Animas River Flood courtesy of Jim McCann pictured on Bill Butler's (aka Durango Bill's) website (http://www.durangobill.com/AnimasRiverFlood.html). No copyright.

Then there is the follow-up story on the small stone which this author believes has an unexpectedly tragic ending—a dog (or some other unfortunate quadruped) was struck by a brilliant flash of lightning with a deep rumbling clap of thunder (quadruped + strike + lightning) [ ] which scared the residue ("shit?") out of the surprised elephant [ ] and caused the bird(s) to fly away across the inundated land [ ].

Do elephants really leave much "residue" behind? You'd better believe it! This has been verified by Mr. Jeffery Stanton, former keeper of the Albuquerque, New Mexico ABQ BioPark elephants who told the author that elephants indeed do poop a lot when scared. Fake photograph adapted by Ronald Stewart from https://www.snopes.com/fact-check/feces-of-death/. No copyright.

The "Elephant Slabs", therefore, are not modern hoaxes, cattle brands, or cowboy doodlings (as believed by some), but rather, are actual written records of a pre-historic event—monsoon rains, lightning strikes, floods and elephant poop! The significance of these "Elephant Slabs" is that they are probably THE EARLIEST (CIRCA 1312 CE) WRITTEN DESCRIPTION OF A PREHISTORIC FLOOD IN THE WESTERN HEMISPHERE.

Prehistoric Jar—The Elephant Pitcher

Ronald Stewart's interpretation of what the Indian potter was thinking:
There's an unwanted monster feasting and defecating in my cornfield!
Top of jar was reconstructed by Ronald Stewart, adapted from an illustration of a "prehistoric jar with an elephant decoration" from E.B. "Ted" Sayles, *Fantasies of Gold,* Tucson: University of Arizona Press, 1968, p. 92.

A pitcher with a cornstalk and a raised-tail elephant figure on it, which is said to be from approximately the same time period as the elephant slabs, was discovered in the Montezuma Valley, to the northwest of Flora Vista ("within sight of the spot from which the Elephant Slabs came" stated Wright and Sayles). According to Frederick Bennett Wright (1873-1922), the pitcher was found about 1885—taken from a ruin. E. B. Sayles asked: "Does the pot have any relationship to the Elephant Slabs?[75] The answer is an emphatic "YES"—the time period is right, the elephants were in the neighborhood, and they would have gorged themselves on cornstalks, given the chance! The pitcher was last known to be in the possession of Benjamin W. and Jeannette Ritter of Durango, Colorado.[76] This author has interpreted the design from the potter's perspective as "*there's an unwanted monster feasting and defecating in my cornfield!*" It is clear from this that the Emperor (or his designated caravan manager) allowed the elephants to not only graze in valleys to the north of the San Juan River, but to ravage some of the Pueblo Indian cornfields as well. Of course, this would have caused problems for the Emperor and made his entourage unwelcome guests in Pueblo country—so they moved on, perhaps quicker than anticipated.

The only indication that part of the Emperor's caravan might have traveled north to visit Mesa Verde's cliff dwellings near the Mancos River Valley is the discovery of this elephant decorated pitcher in a Montezuma Valley ruin. If he was guided to the abandoned cliff dwellings, perhaps by a former resident, he would have been amazed by the numerous rooms and kivas (like those in the Cliff Palace) tucked high inside elevated overhangs in the extensive cliff face.

Excavated Cliff Palace, Mesa Verde National Park, public domain photo.

After following the Animas River and then the San Juan River a short ways, the caravan of humans, camels and elephants soon would have passed Hogback Mountain and reached the site of a curious pinnacle. As they trekked west down the westward flowing San Juan River, through the river's verdant valley, they would have passed this amazing monolith which every modern day tourist recognizes as "Shiprock". What the Emperor thought it looked like went unrecorded, but the Navajo Indians later (after they moved down from the North and East) thought of it as *"Tsé Bit'a'í"*, the "winged rock".

Views from below and above of "*Tsé Bit'a'í*" "Rock with Wings" or "Shiprock", New Mexico. (top) by Bowie Snodgrass. Both Wikipedia images are in the public domain.

South of Shiprock there are even more spectacular natural phenomenon known as The Bisti/De-Na-Zin Wilderness and Ah-Shi-Sle-Pah.

The Bisti/De-Na-Zin Wilderness. Photograph by John Fowler from Placitas, NM. Licensed under the Creative Commons Attribution 2.0 Generic license.

Ah-Shi-Sle-Pah hoodoos June 28, 2010. Photograph by John Fowler from Placitas, NM. Licensed under Creative Commons Attribution 2.0 Generic license.

The Bisti/De-Na-Zin Wilderness is a rolling landscape of badlands which offers some of the most unusual scenery found in the Four Corners Region. Time and natural elements have etched a fantasy world of strange rock formations made of interbedded sandstone, shale, mudstone, coal, and silt. The weathering of the sandstone forms hoodoos— weathered rock in the form of pinnacles, spires, cap rocks, and other unusual forms. Fossils occur in this sedimentary landform.[77]

Like the Bisti and De-Na-Zin wildernesses a short distance northwest, Ah-Shi-Sle-Pah … is a little known region of fantastic eroded rocks in the high desert of northwest New Mexico, a generally flat, sandy and uninhabited land drained by shallow washes that eventually meet the San Juan River. Some of the land [today] is part of the Navajo Indian Reservation, and other areas are used for oil and gas drilling, but most is empty, yet access is quite easy since a network of dirt roads crisscross the desert, many in good condition except after recent rainfall when some become impassable. The [area] is centered on Ah-Shi-Sle-Pah Wash, a minor drainage running through a wide, barren valley but lined to the north and south by a strip of eroded cliffs, ravines and badlands containing innumerable hoodoos, balanced rocks and other strange formations, plus much petrified wood including stumps still in an upright position, complete with roots. The rocks (a mixture of sandstones, mudstones and shales, from the Fruitland Formation) have a great variety of colors, especially distinctive being the brown-ochre of the badlands and yellow-orange of some of the hoodoos; other dominant shades are grey-white of the mud hills lining the valley floor, and deep black both of the badlands higher up, and scattered coal beds closer to the wash. Although the formations extend for 6 miles, the best and most easily reached section of the [area] next to the official trailhead is just 1.5 miles across so the majority can be seen in half a day; other interesting areas on the north side of the valley and downstream to the west would need a day or more to explore fully. Besides the petrified wood, the Ah-Shi-Sle-Pah region is a fruitful source of animal fossils, and many dinosaur bones have been collected here over the last hundred years; some may still be seen in situ.[78]

Whether the Emperor of Mali actually explored these distant desert hiking sites, where dinosaurs once roamed, cannot be ascertained—but anything is possible. After all he was a pretty courageous, if mysterious, explorer.

Eventually, thoroughly awed, these intrepid 14th century tourists from the Mali Empire would have continued down the San Juan Valley into Utah—going ever westward by north westward, just north of today's popular "Four Corners Monument" which identifies the spot where the present-day states of Utah, Colorado, Arizona and New Mexico meet at the Ute Mountain Ute Tribe's and the Navajo Nation's Reservation boundaries. Modern-day tourists love it. The Navajo Parks and Recreation Department maintains the site and around the monument, local Navajo and Ute artisans sell colorful souvenirs such as turquoise and silver jewelry, dreamcatchers—and food, such as Indian fry bread and Navajo Tacos. Yum Yum, Abu Bakr II didn't know what he was missing!

Four Corners Monument., Photograph by Vicki Watkins from USA. Licensed under the Creative Commons Attribution 2.0 Generic license.

Petroglyph of an Elephant, Near Bluff, Utah

Other rock art in the San Juan Valley of Utah, has been identified as Columbian Mammoths. "Rock art depictions of proboscids at the Upper Sand Island site along the San Juan River near Bluff, Utah, appear to be "bona fide".[76] 120 km away from this site, in the Escalante River drainage of southern Utah, is Bechan [*bay-chawn*] Cave, where archaeological investigations uncovered over 225 cubic meters of mammoth dung, and radiocarbon dating showed that mammoths may have survived on the Colorado Plateau until about 11 000 BP [before present]. This provides a minimum age for the creation of the mammoth petroglyph at Upper Sand Island. Bechan Cave is big enough to shelter a herd of mammoths. It is 52 meters long and 31 meters wide. Two paleontologists, Dr. Jim Mead and Dr. Larry Agenbroad, found a layer of mammoth dung from 10 centimeters to 40 centimeters deep. The scientists named it Bechan, which means 'big dung' in Navajo. Dung from many other animals was mixed with the mammoth dung. Horses, camels, deer, ground sloths, and many other animals shared this region with the Columbian mammoths. But some whole mammoth droppings as big as bowling balls also were found and these allowed the scientists to determine that most of the dung had indeed come from mammoths. "The mammoth dung had hair that matched that of wooly mammoths from Siberia, and the grass in the dung had long fibers, like that in elephant dung." The mammoths' diet consisted of mostly grasses, as well as sedge, birch, spruce, rose, sagebrush and even cactus spines [could some of these plants make the Emperor's elephants sick?]. This was a sign that they got their food from a large, dry area with a few rivers where wetland plants could grow, just like the habitat in the mountains near Bechan Cave today.

Although a couple of scientists have identified petroglyphs in the upper and lower Sand Island area of the San Juan Valley near Bluff, Utah, as probable petroglyphs of mammoths, stating that: "The proboscidean images clearly testify pictorially to the co-existence of early Paleo-americans with now-extinct Pleistocene megafauna ..., since these elephantid petroglyphs contain "distinctive inverted V-shaped bifurcation at the tip of the trunk. Mammalogists refer to this as 'fingers.' As appendages of prehension, they aid proboscideans in grasping food during foraging activities." However, African savanna elephants also have similar double prehensile digits, begging the question—could some of these images actually be early fourteenth century depictions of the Mali Emperor/Explorer's elephants?[79] Samuel Hubbard suggested in his 1925 *The Doheny Scientific Expedition to the Hava Supai Canyon, Northern Arizona, October and November, 1924*, Oakland Museum, Oakland, CA. that the image of the Sand Island petroglyph was in reality a wooly rhinoceros. He stated that: "All the 'rhino' character is present. The menacing horn; the prehensile upper lip; the short tail; the heavy body and short legs, all suggest a 'rhino' about to charge. This is the first time it has ever been known that prehistoric man in America was contemporary with the rhinoceros". Others have seen a mastodon, or even a bear with a fish in its mouth. This petroglyph, near Bluff, Utah, however, may be relevant to the Emperor's prehistoric traveling caravan:

San Juan River Elephant Petroglyph

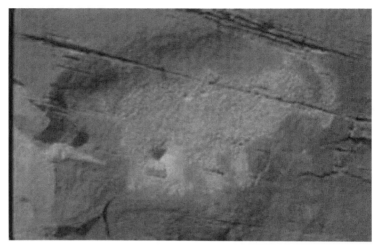

Photograph by Dell Crandall, 1999

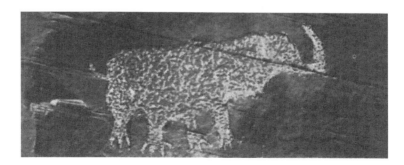

A trumpeting Mali elephant petroglyph near Sand Island, Bluff, Utah? Photograph by Mr. Kelly, Grand Junction, Colorado, pre-1925, The outline of the figure was so faint that he was obliged to chalk it to secure a satisfactory photograph. Both photographs from Peter Faris, Rock Art blog. http://rockartblog.blogspot.com/2015/01/. "The material on this site is copyrighted and is the result of 30 years of study by the author, and involved considerable travel and materials. You are welcome to download or use anything you find here but please be sure to give the correct citation (© *year*, Peter Faris, RockArtBlog)".

Following this well-watered valley westward, the Emperor would have reached a point where the river was so constricted that he could not justify staying close to it.

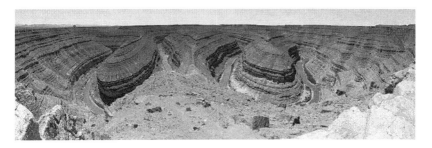

San Juan River winds through a narrow steep canyon in present-day Goosenecks State Park, Utah. Photograph by Gernot Keller, London, August 20, 2009. Licensed under the Creative Commons Attribution 3.0 Unported license.

His scouts would have had even worse news—the canyon bound San Juan River joined an even larger river (Colorado River) which flowed into an even deeper canyon—a GRAND CANYON. Perhaps this time no friendly natives appeared out of the dust of the Colorado Plateau to guide him. Without them, he would have been at a complete loss as to what to do. His advisors likewise probably wouldn't agree on a plan of action at first. Nevertheless, Chinle and Laguna Creek Valleys, leading south and west, probably seemed to be the better alternative, despite their small size and despite possible encounters with native fauna such as wolves, coyotes, rattlesnakes and mountain lions. Mountain lions, in particular, would have been gastronomically interested in any baby or small animals traveling with the caravan. The route would have looked dangerously dry and undesirable, but there were interesting natural features to be seen nearby.

"Mountain Lion Petroglyph", photo credit: Petrified Forest Ranger. Petrified Forest National Park, Arizona. Public domain.

Located near the San Juan Valley, just east of the forbidding "goosenecks" of the river, a sight worth a side trip for the Emperor would have been the strange natural phenomenon known today as the *"Mexican Hat"*. The curious name comes from a strange sombrero-shaped rock outcropping. The rock measures sixty feet (18 m) wide by twelve feet (3.7 m). Its sandstone tower is an eroded remnant of a sea sediment deposit dating back to the dinosaur era, or earlier. If they saw it, Abu Bakr II's people probably discussed among themselves just how the "hat" could remain balanced so perfectly on top its eroding sandstone base. Other nearby sights that might have caught the travelers' attention include the Valley of the Gods (similar to Monument Valley) and the Muley Point vista of cliffs with the San Juan River far below (similar to the Grand Canyon). One could truly feel alone and abandoned in this part of the Southwest as the sandstone mesas and canyons seem to stretch to infinity.

Mexican Hat, Utah. This photograph is in the public domain.

Abandoned ancestral Pueblo Indian villages, tucked away beneath cliffs, such as Keet Seel (Kawestima) and Betatakin ("House Built on a Ledge" in Navajo, or *Talastima*, "Place of the Corn Tassel" in Hopi), would have been close enough for popular sightseeing—just as they are today. A map of the Laguna Creek region of northern Arizona demonstrates that the probable route of the Emperor's caravan was not totally dry. Creek water, as well as water from springs and pools was available, if not abundant.

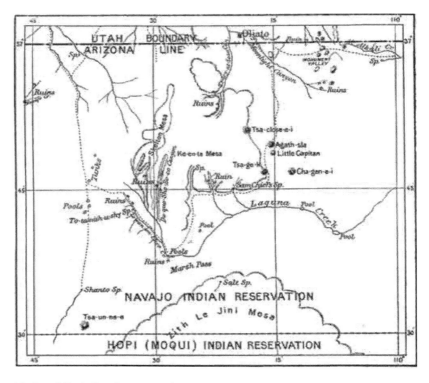

National Park Service map of Laguna Creek. Public domain.

Moenkopi Wash, Arizona, from Wikimedia Commons. Public domain.

160

Here, along the creeks and washes, the Emperor and his caravan would have run across one of the Hopi Pueblo Indian villages, known as Moenkopi. Perhaps he also visited other Hopi pueblos around First, Second and Third Mesas.

Moenkopi village, Moenkopi Wash, Coconino County, Arizona, Echo Cliffs quadrangle. August, 1914. Digital File:ghe00277 ID. Gregory, H.E. 277. The horses and fences are later additions—the buildings, however, may be on the site of original windowless, adobe structures. From:http://libraryphoto.cr.usgs.gov/htmllib/free1.htm, in public domain.

Continuing on over the Hopi Trail westward toward Havasu Creek, Abu Bakr II would have traveled along Moenkopi Wash, and part of the Little Colorado River Valley. Perhaps he even traveled farther afield on side trips to see Monument Valley, Wupatki ruins, dormant Sunset Crater Volcano (which had erupted around 1085 CE), Walnut Canyon cliff dwellings and Meteor Crater. Since cliff overhangs and caves would have been sighted in the nearby canyons, possibly it was finally agreed that there protection from the elements (heat and haboobs [dust storms]) could be obtained—the animals, however, would have to forge for themselves.

"The Elephants are Sick and Angry"

Since African elephants can consume three hundred pounds of vegetation a day, it would have been vital for them to be led through a highly nutritious plant environment. But that is not part of Northeastern Arizona's biotic communities. The Colorado Plateau (Great Basin Desert) and Arizona/New Mexico Plateau biotic communities consist of desert shrubs—small leafed, hardy plants, frequently with spines, or thorns.

West and East Mitten Buttes and Merrick Butte, Monument Valley, Arizona, on the Colorado Plateau of northeastern-most Arizona. They are sculpted from Permian-age shales, sandstones, and siltstones that formed more than 250 million years ago. Notice the sparse vegetation. Photograph by Jon Sullivan, from Wikimedia Commons, Public Domain .

For lack of sufficient grasses, the elephants, like their ancient mammoth cousins probably turned to needle infested cactus, cholla and ocotillo, but also could have consumed plants such

(left) Cactus, (center) Cholla (right) Ocotillo, photographs courtesy of Joanne Stewart

as locoweed (crazyweed), jimson weed (datura) and silver-leaf nightshade (known to be poisonous to elephants by Mr. Jeffery Stanton, former Elephant Keeper at Albuquerque's ABQ BioPark Zoo).

Datura (D. wrightii) known as Sacred Datura, or metaloides, jimsonweed or devil's weed, a perennial herb, is found in all the major deserts of the American Southwest. Photograph courtesy of Joanne Stewart.

As a result of ingesting these needle infested and poisonous plants, the elephants would not have been able to function. Some of them probably were not only fatally "sick", but "angry" (hallucinating?) as well. Possibly, the whole caravan ground to a halt until a decision to turn back or to proceed westward through dry canyon country could be made.

Somewhere near today's Four Corners, Arizona, someone of Mali's "Secret Society" (court official, noble, merchant, priest or blacksmith), literate in Mandinka, the language of Mali (or possibly some other related West African language) supposedly inscribed a petroglyph record of this event on a cave wall. The translated inscription allegedly reads *"The elephants are sick and angry. At present there are considerable (or many) sick elephants."* A petroglyph of an elephant and a bird accompanies the inscription. Rock art and runes found in this cave near the Four Corners of Arizona picture conditions in the desert. Below are two of the lines of the Arizona inscriptions. Upside down mountains indicated just the opposite—flatlands, i.e., Arizona desert. Notice that the bird is different than the ones depicted on the Flora Vista "elephant slabs"—perhaps indicating a different author.

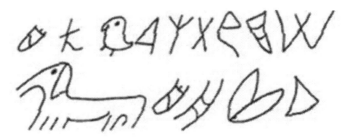

From "Islam in Early North and South America" by Clyde-Ahmad Winters and *The Big Book of Mysteries* by Lionel and Patricia Fanthorpe, Dundurn Press, Toronto, Canada, 2010, page 139

1st line:— *"ga-gya kpa-nde -ngbe—ka-go-ne"* translated as: *"The desert is hot. Birds are numerous—white (ka) and called go"* [could *"go"* mean "gull", similar to the California sea gulls that perhaps attacked the insects that were plaguing the Utah Mormons centuries later in 1848, or was it the name of an African bird with which the explorers were already familiar?]

2nd line: – *"elephant-ga-ka. Bi-kpa"* translated as *"The elephants are sick and angry. At present sick elephants are considerable [or many]"* [alternate translation: *elephants are unwell and behaving badly as if they are hallucinating*].

Was this the Emperor's plea for help from Allah or from some ancient Mali god, or was he just venting his frustration? Did this event near the present-day New Mexico-Utah-Arizona border mean the end of the journey?

Did the Mali Emperor also dispatch a scouting party riding elephants through central Arizona to find a better way westward?

At Palatki, west of Sedona, Arizona, in the Coconino National Forest, there is an inscription which supposedly has been translated from Mandinka to English. It was found near the ruins of cliff dwellings, but might not be related to them. This inscription (possibly made by a literate person in a scouting party) seems to describe the picturesque setting where the Palatki inscription and cave dwellings were found:

Palatki pictograph copied by Ronald Stewart

Be   su i se   Se Gyo / Jo

The possible English translation is as follows:
"Exist here a superior place of habitation.
Make (this) place a success, consecrated to the Divinity"

from Dr. Clyde Winters, *Ancient African Writing Systems and Knowledge* blog, June 19, 2014, "African Origin American Mounds"

Another possible elephantid (or mountain lion) petroglyph was found in central Arizona. This petroglyph was discovered near Mayer, Arizona, by Ekkehart Malotki, who stated that it "is surrounded by imagery typically produced by late pre-Historic farmers between 600 and 1450 CE"[80]

Ronald Stewart's line drawing of Mayer, Arizona, petroglyph

Ekkehart Malotki and others have researched petroglyphs in Utah and Arizona that appear to be Ice Age mammoths rhinos, or mountain lions, making it difficult to identify historic elephant petroglyphs such as those that the Native Americans recorded when the Emperor's caravan passed by.[81]

"Chicos, Prietos y Feos" or "Small, Dark and Unattractive People"

The Hopi describe themselves as *Hopituh Shi-nu-mu* "The Peaceful People". Eventually, perhaps in late August or September, during the 16 day snake dance ceremonies, the Emperor would have taken a side trip to visit the Hopi Pueblo Indians on their mesas in northern Arizona.

Line of a dozen Hopi snake priests singing songs and prayers before the kiva at the pueblo of Oraibi, Arizona, 1898 (CHS-4662).jpg. Photograph by George Wharton James, 1858—1923 Wikimedia Commons. Public domain.

A Hopi legend asserts that to the West, The Great Spirit "gave the black race of people the Guardianship of the water. They were to learn the teachings of the water which is the chief of the elements, being the most humble and the most powerful."[82] Did Abu Bakr II tell the Hopi that he had just come westward after conquering the humbling and powerful Atlantic Ocean, and that he was following rivers westward in hopes of crossing the next ocean in order to circumnavigate the watery world?

Statue of Padre Garcés at Saint Thomas Mission in Yuma, Arizona. https://southwestphotojournal.com/2015/01/25/southwest-spanish-missions-brought-the-gospels-light-to-the-rim-of-christendom-helped-the-natives-carve-a-livelihood-from-the-land-and-written-history-began/yuma35/. No copyright.

While trying to convert the Hopi natives in 1776, Fray Francisco Hermenegildo Tomás Garcés stated that: "In this pueblo there are two types of people and two languages spoken: the first has to do with color and size (stature) of the *Indios y Indias* [men and women]; the second is evident in their diverse method of singing (chanting). Some are *claro* [fair skinned] and *rubio* [somewhat fair-haired and well-disposed]; the others are *chicos* [small], *prietos* [very black] and *feos* [unattractive].[83] Fray Garcés had already mentioned Apaches, Navajos and Utes in his "*Diario*", so these blackish people were definitely not any of those tribes, which leaves only one possibility—their ancestors were the Africans (perhaps short people like the pygmy-like Tellem) who were left behind in Northeastern Arizona to care for the sick elephants.

Such a small group probably would have sought protection at Hopi from the more aggressive Tartar/Athapascan speaking Navajos as they infiltrated the northeastern Arizona region. The Native Americans of Hopi, probably, would have welcomed the addition of these black warriors to their defenses.

In the Hopi Medicine wheel of Hopi Prophecy, "West holds the spirit, water, the color blue or black, and 'black-skinned peoples'...."[84] [author's underlining] Could the Hopi small, black Twin War Gods be connected to the *chicos, prietos y feos* of Garcés? Wilson Poola, a Hopi of Tewa descent, told the author in 2015 that there had been black people at Hopi in the past, but he believes that they migrated elsewhere.

Public domain photo of Hopi Pueblo, Arizona: "In this pueblo there are two types of people and two languages spoken: the first has to do with color and size (stature) of the men and women [*Indios y Indias*]; the second is evident in their diverse method of singing (chanting). Some are fair skinned [*claro*] and somewhat fair-haired [*rubio*] and well disposed; the others are small [*chicos*], dark [*prietos*] and unattractive [*feos*]. " (described by Fray Francisco Garcés in his "Diario page 74" and translated for the author by Joseph P. Sanchez, Ph. D., Director of the Spanish Colonial Research Center, University of New Mexico)[83]

Armond de Quatrefages, an anthropologist at the Museum of National History in Paris, in *Introduction a L'Etudes des Races Humaines*, noted that there were small numbers of Blacks in isolated areas like in Arizona and New Mexico— the Indians and Blacks spoke different languages,"[85] Does this observation mean that some of the Mali explorers really did get left behind near the Arizona-New Mexico border to be caretakers of the sick elephants, and that their descendants were still near Arizona Indian villages in the 1400's, 1500's, 1600's, 1700's and 1800's?

171

It has been said that "perhaps the best account of what [Spanish explorer Fray Marcos de] Niza had to say is contained in two contemporary letters, one written August 23, 1539 by Bishop Juan de Zumárraga and the other by Fray Gerónimo Ximénez de San Esteban ... October 9, 1539, to Fray Tomás de Villanueva in Burgos." Bishop Zumárraga, commenting on what Marcos de Niza saw and was told, stated "There are partridges and cows [bison?], which the father says he saw, and heard a story of camels and dromedaries..." [underlining by author]

Fray Ximénez de San Esteban stated that de Niza "traveled over 500 leagues through inhabited territory [Eastern Arizona] and at the end of this passed through a desert for more than sixty leagues, and at the end came to a very well settled country with people of much culture who had cities walled about and great houses [Zuni Pueblo?].... *También dicen que en la tierra más adentro hay camellos y elefantes.* (They also say that in the country beyond [or farther inland] [86] [to the north?], there are camels and elephants.)"[87] [underlining by author]

Rodrigo de Albornoz, the Royal Treasurer of New Spain echoed the Franciscans' disclosures when he reported that Marcos de Niza had declared that "of animals there are camels and elephants and cattle,..."[88] [author's underling] so the knowledge of de Niza's revelation was apparently fairly widespread.

Illustration of Fray Marcos de Niza in Arizona by J. Cisneros (Artist) from Southwest Crossroads, "The Journey of Fray Marcos de Niza", website. No copyright listed.

An abstract of Daniel T. Ruff's 1991 *American Anthropologist* article titled "Anthropological Analysis of Exploration Texts: Cultural Discourse and the Ethnological Import of Fray Marcos de Niza's Journey to Cibola" reveal's that:

This article highlights methodological and theoretical presuppositions that have contributed to scholarly neglect and rejection of exploration chronicles such as Fray Marcos de Niza's account of his journey to Cibola [Zuni Pueblo, Arizona and New Mexico region] in 1539. Marcos's relación and similar texts often have been ignored or rejected because of presuppositions about the

"accuracy" of modern anthropological, as opposed
to historical, texts...."[89]

Some anthropologists and archeologists claim that since no
artifacts have been unearthed to support the claims of early
explorers like Fray Marcos de Niza, then their observations
and informants were wrong. Some historical scholars are just
as ignorant. Some of these scholars have maintained that
since Spanish thinking in the 16th century was that North
America was just a peninsula of Asia (as if the Bering Sea
didn't exist between Siberia and Alaska), then Fray Marcos
de Niza was imagining what animals would be found if one
went farther toward Asia. If so, why did he mention
elephants and camels—fauna of Africa—instead of Asian
water buffalo, yak, Siberian tigers or Himalayan yeti (with
polar bear DNA)? Bishop Zumárraga even described them as
Dromedaries, not Asian two humped Bactrian Camels.
Marcos de Niza didn't mention the latter because he was told
what were ahead were elephants and dromedary camels—
African animals, not Asian—in other words, one has to
conclude that they were most likely descended from Abu
Bakr II's "sick and angry" caravan pack animals. Hooray!
Another Spanish record mystery solved! Fray Marcos de
Niza was not a "liar" after all, even if in 1540, Spanish
explorer of New Mexico, Francisco Vásquez de Coronado
(1510-1554) had declared that the friar had "said the truth in
nothing that he reported".

Elephants near the Grand Canyon?

Did the Mali Emperor get a chance to admire the sun drenched cliffs of the Southwest's greatest canyon?

The Colorado River in the Grand Canyon from Bright Angel Plateau looking east, circa 1900-1930 CE, photographed by C.C. (Charles C.) Pierce. Photograph is in the public domain. Released under the CC by Attribution license — http://creativecommons.org/licenses/by/3.0/ Source: University of Southern California Libraries and California Historical Society. Digitally reproduced by the USC Digital Library.

Following the Hopi Trail westward from the Hopi Pueblos, which stretches through the upper part of Havasu Canyon, there may be some evidence for elephants having been near the south rim of the Grand Canyon. Dr. Samuel Dickinson Hubbard, Honorary Curator of Archaeology of the Oakland

Museum, once visited an area of the Grand Canyon known as Havasu Canyon. Hubbard, in his monograph, stated that "Native Americans must have seen elephants. Interestingly, the inscriptions at Havasupai show an elephant striking a man with its trunk"[90] His interpretation is disputed, but perhaps that is because his critics did not know the story of Abu Bakr II's tremendous accomplishment in traversing the deserts of northern Arizona. Could the Mali elephant have been squirting a Native American, or perhaps trying to rescue its handler from the river? But how could elephants traverse such a narrow canyon?

The Havasupai: *Havsuw' Baaja* or "People of the Blue-Green Waters" and The Hualapai: *Hwalbáy* or "People of the tall trees", who were ethnically identical, were the Grand Canyon and southern rim dwellers that the Emperor's caravan would have encountered next. The tribe traditionally relied heavily on agriculture, hunting and gathering as their means of survival. Although living primarily above and inside the Grand Canyon, which consists mostly of harsh terrain, the tribe's lands were also home to some lush vegetation and beautiful waters[91] including waterfalls and pools.

Did the Emperor's remaining elephants get to splash around in these? Did an Indian see them do this near the top of Havasu canyon and later tried to explain this humorous scene to others down in the lower reaches of the canyon by drawing them a picture?

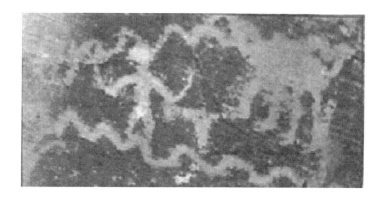

Following the Tobocobe Trail to where it intersects with Lee Canyon, Samuel Hubbard photographed a petroglyph of a man (standing in water?) supposedly fighting with an elephant (standing on land?) in Havasu Canyon—or was the elephant just squirting someone, as this author believes? This photograph is in the public domain.

Do the splayed toes mean that it's not really an elephant? This author believes that the petroglyph is probably another "show and tell" when a Havasupai Indian drew a picture for someone farther down the canyon of what he witnessed in the creek or near one of the waterfall pools farther up in Havasu Creek. So many questions go unanswered.

Line drawing of elephant figure made in Havasu Canyon by Samuel Dickinson Hubbard, May 5, 1923 CE, from the Doheny Scientific Expedition Main Report. Public domain.

July 9, 2009 public domain photograph of Havasu Falls, Havasupai Reservation, Arizona, by Gonzo fan2007, from Wikimedia Commons.

Circa 1899 photograph by George Wharton James, in the public domain. Two Havasupai Indian women sit and stand in front of a native dwelling in Havasu Canyon. A "*kathak*", a large conical basket, lies on the ground. Another one has been strapped to the back of the person on the left. A woven water container lies in the center while the person on the right appears to be weaving another basket. The small, dome-shaped dwelling is formed of a lattice of sticks covered with thatching. Public domain. .http://digitallibrary.usc.edu/cdm/ref/collection/p15799coll65/id/16315

The Yavapai—"people of the sun" (from *enyaeva* "sun" + *pai* "people")[92] "were mainly hunter-gatherers, following an annual round, migrating to different areas to follow the ripening of different edible plants, although some tribes supplemented this with small scale cultivation of the "three sisters"—maize, squash, and beans—in fertile streambeds. The early Yavapai did dances such as the Mountain Spirit Dance, War Dances, Victory Dances and Social Dances. The Mountain Spirit dance was a masked dance which was used for guidance or healing of a sick person, the masked dancers impersonated Mountain Spirits. The Yavapai lived in brush shelters called a *Wa'm bu nya:va* (Wom-boo-nya-va). In summer, shelters were often simple lean-tos without walls. During winter months, closed huts (called *uwas*) would be built of ocotillo branches or other wood and covered with animal skins, grasses, bark, and/or dirt, though in the Colorado River area, Đo:lkabaya (Western Yavapai Band) built *Uwađ a'mađva*, which was a rectangular hut, that had dirt piled up against its sides, and a flat roof. Other shelter was often sought in caves or abandoned pueblos to escape the cold."[93] After seeing the Pueblo Indian lifestyle of the Rio Grande, the Emperor would not have been impressed, yet these Colorado River Indian tribes had managed to successfully adapt to the harsh conditions of the hot climate and dry desert.

"Mojave or *Hamakhaave*, which means 'beside the water' are Indians who inhabit the middle reaches of the Colorado River south of the Grand Canyon. Mojave people built a couple of types of houses. Near the Colorado River, the Mojaves lived in thatched huts raised off the ground by stilts, to protect against summer floods. Farther from the river, Mojave people built sturdier earthen houses, which were made of a wooden frame packed with clay. The thick earth walls kept this kind of house cool in the heat and warm in the cold, making it good shelter in the desert. Mojave people didn't wear much clothing—men wore only loincloths and women wore knee-length skirts. Shirts were not necessary in Mojave culture, but the Mojaves sometimes wore rabbit-skin robes at night when the weather became cooler."

Mojave Indians, by German artist Heinrich Balduin Möllhausen published in the Indian Report for the "Reports of Explorations and Surveys, to Ascertain the Most Practicable and Economical Route For a Railroad from the Mississippi River to the Pacific Ocean." of the 35th Parallel. Lithograph by T. Sinclair. Public domain.

Unlike most Indian tribes, the Mojaves never wore moccasins. They either went barefoot or wore sandals. Some of the Mojaves had facial tattoos and also painted their faces and bodies for special occasions. They used different colors and patterns for war paint, religious ceremonies, and festive decoration. Many Mojave people also painted horizontal white or yellow stripes on their hair. The Mojaves were farming people. They planted crops of corn, beans, and pumpkins. They especially liked to trade corn and beans for shell beads from the Pacific coast, which they used to make jewelry. Mojave men also hunted rabbits and small game and fished in the rivers, while women gathered nuts, fruits, and herbs. Favorite Mojave recipes included baked beans, hominy, and flat breads made from corn and bean flour. They traveled on foot or sometimes by raft, if they wanted to cross the river."[94]

Primitive Transportation—Mojave, 1907 photograph by E. S. Curtis, in the public domain The Mojave and Yuma tribal members were expert fishers who used nets and baskets to catch fish. They traveled along the Colorado River on rafts and poles to different fishing locations as well as transported goods across the Colorado River.

The River Yuman [Patayan, Quechan], who inhabited the area around the lower Colorado and Gila Rivers, farmed the floodplain. Annual flooding of the rivers deposited silt and naturally irrigated the land, making for fertile soil. They lived in small settlements above the floodplain where they established rectangular, open-sided dwellings. In the period after the floods until fall the people farmed small plots of land owned by each family, living in small dome-shaped *wickiup* shelters. The Havasupai, mostly due to their location in the Grand Canyon, practiced more extensive farming and lived a peaceful lifestyle. The others, like the River Yumans, were warlike in nature. The Upland Yuman were closer in lifestyle to the desert cultures of the southwestern United States. While they did some subsistence farming, providing for the basic needs of the farmer, they generally practiced a hunter-gatherer lifestyle.[95]

A Yuma Home. 1907 Photograph by E. S. Curtis, in the public domain.

The Emperor's caravan probably encountered many birds along the Colorado River which undoubtedly reminded them of home—were they getting homesick yet?

American Egrets roosting and nesting on the Colorado River Indian Reservation near Parker, Yuma County, Arizona. Photograph by Charles O'Rear for the Environmental Protection Agency's Project DOCUMERICA, May 1972, US National Archives. Public domain.

Baja California Coincidences?

Following the Colorado River to its mouth, then, crossing the Baja California peninsula with the help of local Yuma Indian or other guides, perhaps the Malians had gotten to California before the Spanish, just like they did in Texas, New Mexico and Arizona. Once they reached the salt water of the Gulf of California at the mouth of the Colorado River, the Emperor would have realized that a new ocean was close enough to successfully complete his adventure, but the decision was, of course, the Emperor's to make. His scouts, possibly with the aid of local Indians, eventually found a suitable trail on the east side of Baja California, probably up Arroyo El Volcán, named for the cold water geyser which erupts periodically. Today, pickup trucks or four-wheel drive vehicles can travel four miles northeast from El Marmol [Spanish for onyx] to Arroyo El Volcán where soda springs and a rare cold water geyser are creating future onyx deposits.

To locate the site, set the odometer on your vehicle at the abandoned El Marmol schoolhouse ruin (only one ever built of onyx) and proceed on the road to the northeast to a fork at Mile 2.0. Then turn right and drop down a steep hill to the bottom in the El Volcán arroyo at Mile 4.0. The site of the geyser/spring is up the arroyo (right, south) almost half a mile. The pools of water and mineral deposits provide scenes of interest. A hiker can get a sense of what it took for elephants and camels to traverse the Baja California peninsula's arroyos. The soda powered geyser is said to gush a sixty foot fountain of water once a month. The question is:

Did Abu Bakr II's Indian guides time it right for him to see this natural wonder?

Baja California's El Volcán—"The geyser at its top erupts for several minutes once a month [at present] forcing water 60 feet high. The action is created by soda action and not heat, so it is a cold water geyser." https://www.tacomaworld.com/threads/baja-californias-onyx-schoolhouse-and-cold-water-geyser.89694/ No copyright listed.

El Volcán arroyo led over a pass in the peninsular cordillera to present-day Arroyo Agua Dulce and a waterhole. David Kier described the situation travelers faced in journeying through Baja California:

"Water sources in the desert are more valuable than gold when one is thirsty. In the not too distant past, traveling the Baja California peninsula was only possible if water could be found at intervals that were reachable before one succumbs to the heat.... The Indians used these water sources.... Water sources needed to be close enough to each other to be reached in a day's travel.... The first European discovery of Agua Dulce was made by Jesuit Padre Wenceslaus Linck on March 3, 1766,... Agua Dulce appears to have been named by Father Serra, as seen in his diary of 1769...."

But, by naming the waterhole "Agua Dulce" for its "sweet water", Father Serra ignored the fact that Cochimi Indians had already named it "Keita", the same name as Emperors Abu Bakr's and Musa's family/dynasty name. Coincidence? This author thinks not! This is also the same name of the Mali Republic's (1960) first president—Modibo Keïta

(4 June 1915 – 16 May 1977) as well as that of a recent president, Ibrahim Boubacar Keïta (born

29 January 1945). "Keita" was apparently a name to be remembered.

The spring of *Keita* or *Agua Dulce* is in a gully, in the arroyo of Agua Dulce. 1963 photograph by Howard Gulick. Special Collections & Archives, UC San Diego, La Jolla, 92093-0175 (https://lib.ucsd.edu/sca). Used under fair use provision.

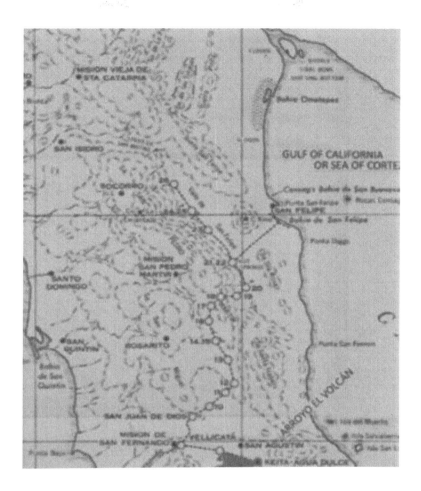

Arroyo El Volcán, Keita/Agua Dulce spring fed waterhole (bottom) and water sources along the later Spanish mission road, based on Howard Gulick's 1954 *El Camino Real* Map from David Kier on Bajabound.com and altered by Ronald Stewart.

The route of the Emperor's party, therefore, can easily be traced from the west coast of the Gulf of California, up Arroyo El Volcán, over the *cordillera*, resting and refreshing themselves at the Keita Spring's pool for numerous days

189

while scouts searched south and north for a protected harbor with large trees nearby. After a two day minimum journey, the caravan would have reached the refreshing waters of Rio San Fernando, the site of the future mission of San Fernando Velicatá, where someone capable of writing with symbols inscribed a message. The symbol "M" for "mountains" is very clear—the rest is not—except that the "j^u|T" probably was written by the "J"es"uit" priest Wenceslaus Linck who chose Velicatá for the site of the future mission in 1766. Whether most of the symbols are Mandinka or Jesuit is unknown.

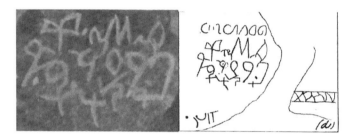

(left) Portion of a petroglyph panel at San Fernando Velicatá, as photographed by Arthur North (1908b:125). (right) The petroglyph as drawn by Ruth Haulenbeek. Regarding these carvings, Arthur North stated: "until some method of deciphering these petroglyphs is discovered, all that can be predicated of the earliest Californians is that they were sufficiently advanced in civilization to clothe themselves and to employ an alphabet." From Echos of a Writing System in Prehistoric Baja California" website, posted on March 5, 2015 by Beau Anderson.

After writing or observing the mysterious inscription, it would not have taken much longer for the camels to follow a trail to the west to the treeless, sand strewn Pacific Coast, but finding a suitable harbor and forest needed for shipbuilding probably took longer.

A bay without nearby suitable trees for ship construction, from Bahía Todos Santos, Wikimedia Commons, Ensenada Bay, by Gabrial Flores Romero. licensed under the Creative Commons Attribution 2.0 Generic license.

Finding a source of fresh, potable water, as opposed to salty marine water, would also have been necessary for restocking their supplies. That's two indications as to which direction, north or south, the Emperor's party took when it reached the Pacific Ocean. After his scouts looked over the seacoast in both directions, they would have concluded that NORTH seemed the most desirable.

There are some springs located east of today's Ensenada called *Ojos Negros*. Were they so named because the two oval, almost swampy pools were dark, or because they looked like "Black Eyes" as some claim (1864 map)?

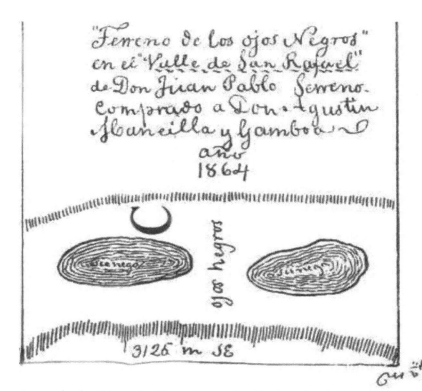

A map in the Zárate Archives, Ensenada, Mexico, dated 1864, showing the two oval-shaped swamps that gave their name to the Ojos Negros valley. https://ponce.sdsu.edu/effect_of_groundwater_pumping.html. Public domain.

Or were they so named by the local Indians (and later translated into Spanish) because in 1312+, some Black People once camped at the springs, which may mean that they really should have been translated as *ojos de los negros*? It is unclear as to the original meaning, but would the

Emperor's party have passed up a chance to drink spring water, or bathe in the nearby *Agua Caliente* (hot water) that his scouts easily would have discovered with the help of local Indians?

Ojos Negros Image from dvd ojos negros 1.wmv. No copyright.

A local tourist site, located 17 miles south of present-day Ensenada, was named La Bufadora (the snorter) by the Spanish. The Emperor's scouts would have urged him to cast his eyes on the largest sea geyser, or blowhole, in North America, a striking natural feature located in the Punta Banda Peninsula. The sea geyser shoots water out of a sea cave more than 100 feet into the air. Legend describes this natural phenomenon as the angry snorts of a whale that got stuck inside the underwater cave and is trying to get out. The spout of sea water is the result of air, trapped in a sea cave or crevasse, exploding upwards. Air is forced into the cave by wave action and is released when the water recedes. This interaction not only creates the spout, but a thunderous noise as well. The phenomena repeats every minute or so with its volume depending on the strength of the waves. The Emperor, if he saw it near its maximum spouting and roaring, couldn't help but have been impressed with the sheer power of the geyser.

The rest of this book is based on speculation and assumptions.

Prehistoric Black Californians?

One assumption is that the Emperor decided to stay in Baja California, or Southern California, because of the Black Californians later said to be found there by the Chinese, Spanish and Americans. But there may be several explanations for dark colored people in Southern California.

The Emperor's caravan (or what was left of it) would have met other Native American bands, and members probably fathered half-breed children while descending the Colorado River Valley and while crossing Baja California peninsula. Between 1769 and 1772, a Franciscan priest baptized approximately 390 Cochimi Indians at San Fernando Velicatá, so the Emperor's party probably would have encountered similar numbers of natives eking out a tenuous living around the various creeks, springs and watering holes of the peninsula about 1312.

"Dieg ueño Woman of Campo" circa 1924, photograph by Edward S. Curtis. public domain photograph.

One has to feel sorry for the angry and hurting elephants—but on the other hand, despite the reduction in elephant numbers, perhaps, finally, a few Malians did reach the Pacific shores of California as seen in these pictures of their possible descendants. The author cannot confirm that there were descendants of the Emperor's exploratory party—but, other writers have alluded to that possibility:

Jean François de Galaup, comte de Lapérouse (1741- 1788), a French explorer, found Blacks in today's California. He called them Ethiopians [a general term at the time for Black Africans].[96] It is said that there were already Blacks in the San Diego area when Hernán Cortés arrived in Baja California. "Further, there are a number of Native American legends," according to "African Ancestry in California" website, "which often appear to be historically accurate, concerning the arrival of early Blacks...," for example, " the first Spanish explorers ... were told by the American Indians that Black men with curly hair made trips from California's shores to the Pacific on missions of trade." As well as "in California, descendnats [sic] of the fierce 'Black Californians'... were a Negroid people of African racial origins" and said by Indian natives to be "the original owners of California and the South west (before the spanish invsion [sic] ... or the creation of the mixed race 'hispanic' ethnic group). It is claimed that many African-Americans in California are of Black Californian ancestry and their great grandparents were among the original Black Californians who were victims of Spanish *Californio* enslavement and Anglo American settler attacks. In fact, the Black Californian fought until the late 1800's to maintain control of their ancestral lands from the settlers."[97]

A 1763 copy (declared fraudulent by some, but probably authentic) of a lost 1418 world map, attributed to Chinese Admiral Zheng He, mentions in Chinese characters that "the skin of the race in this area [west coast of America] is black/red, and feathers are wrapped around their heads and waists".[98] [underlining by author]

A few European painters produced portraits of native American Blacks in the early 1800s, note feathers around head and waist. Public domain image

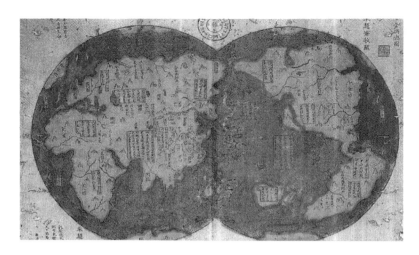

If authentic, Chinese cartographers must have mapped the California shores between 1312 and 1418 noting that some of the inhabitants were "black" as well as "red" with feathers wrapped around head and waist.

Early 17th-century Chinese woodblock print, thought to represent Zheng He's ships (photograph of a work of art that is in the public domain).

The 1763 map copy was purchased from a Shanghai dealer in 2001 by Chinese lawyer and collector, Liu Gang. The map, which is titled a "general chart of the integrated world," in Chinese, is inscribed with the name Mo Yi-tong. I think that we can conclude that the original chart's annotator somehow knew the veracity of what he added to the chart, indicating that there were California coastal Blacks as well as (red ochre covered?) Indians.

Black Indians United claims that:

> For 18 years, Malcolm J. Rogers served as Director of the prestigious Museum of Man in San Diego, California. He was famously known and sought by peers as the "Active Dean of Southwest Archaeology." Aside from conducting studies upon Aboriginal remains,.., his most brilliant claim to fame was to have also conducted a 40 year Forensic Archaeological Study of "The First San Diegans" in North America. In 1958, Malcolm J. Rogers announced publically, that he had confirmed the historic presence of Australo/African Aboriginals as Indigenous Peoples Native to the soil of North America, and had (in fact) been the first San Diegans.... Included by Rogers were, La Jollans, San Diegans, Tribes in Escondido, Encinitas and numerous other areas as 'Black'.... Other explorers having incursions with the same tribal peoples left confirmed accounts the Black aboriginals self-identified as indigenous

and were regarded thusly on account of their descent from populations inhabiting the country from a remote age, prior to conquest, colonization and establishment of present state boundaries.[99]

Paul Barton stated that: "The Black Californian broke up as a nation during the late 1800's after many years of war with the Spanish invaders of the South West, with Mexico and with the U.S. They blended into the Black population of California and their descendants still exist among the millions of Black Californians of today."[100] Diane Blackmon Bailey stated on Lee Bailey's Eurweb's "The History of Queen Califia and the California Blacks" that: "It is now also an archeological fact that the true original people of the Americas included many nations and the Black Californians were one of them as decedents [sic] of... [the] West Africa Manding...."

This author is inclined to believe that some members of the Mali exploration party, with or without their elephants, succeeded in reaching the land of "Queen Califia". According to Reverend Edward Everett Hale, her name originated in a popular sixteenth century romantic novel written by Garci Rodriquez de Montalvo titled *Las Sergas de Esplandián*, and according to the "African Ancestry in California" website: she was said to rule an "island nation" of Amazons, "where gold was the only metal." Hernán Cortés, *conquistador* of Mexico, supposedly even announced to his men that they had reached the land of "Queen Califia".

AN EMBLEM OF AMERICA.

An Emblem of America, 1798, published in London, England, February 1, 1801, by Haines & Son. The British Museum called it an allegorical figure. It is said that the headdress suggests one of the Black California tribes, and the spotted animal skin could be ocelot, lynx or California bobcat. Public domain image.

However, if the Emperor's intention was to continue westward in order to return to his starting point in Mali, then he must have had some ocean going ships built. But where would have been the best harbor for large scale boat building? Was it Bahia San Quintin, where they could fish for bass, bonito and barracuda? Probably not, because it was a shallow bay and there were not suitable trees nearby for shipbuilding—only cardón cactus. There is only one—San

Diego Bay, in California—with its twelve mile long bay protected from storms by a natural breakwater—and trees like the coast live oak, willow and cottonwood, plus palm trees.

Mission Bay Palm Trees. Public domain.

Franciscan priest Junípero Serra later wrote of San Diego Bay as "truly a fine one, and with reason famous."

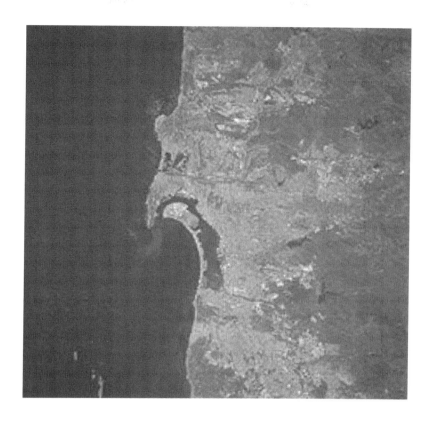

San Diego Bay from Space, NASA - Image courtesy of Earth Sciences and Image Analysis Laboratory, NASA Johnson Space Center: NASA photo STS090-758-17, mission STS090, roll 758, frame 17. Public domain.

Probably not enough ships would have been built by hand to be manned by all of his entourage and those that may have been built, would have been inferior to the original African ones due to lack of proper equipment. Where would his ship carpenters have acquired the metal needed for nails, brackets, hinges, pulleys, etc.? Anchors, of course, could have been made of stone as the Chinese used. Circular stones with donut like holes found along the West Coast of America have been attributed to Chinese fishing and exploratory ships. Since the San Diego region and Baja California lack huge trees readily available for dugout construction, the ships must have been constructed from other designs, possibly previously learned from other Islamic cultures.

Replica of a ship, typical of the 10th–14th centuries in Islamic Iberia. located in Almería, Spain, from Wikipedia, "Ship", which also mentions that there is "great speculation, with historical evidence, that it is possible that Malian sailors may have reached the coast of Pre-Columbian America under the rule of Abubakari II, nearly two hundred years before Christopher Columbus". Olea's public domain photograph.

It can be assumed that regardless of his good intentions, the Emperor failed to reach home. Therefore, he must have died somewhere in his travels. No known monument or inscription has ever been found indicating his place of death. It is conceivable that Abu Bakr II was the first emperor (and perhaps the only emperor, other than Emperor Norton of San Francisco) to have died in America—or what is more probable—out in the Pacific Ocean while trying to be the first to circumnavigate the wide, wide world.

Did the Emperor, himself, make it all the way to Baja California? Did he have more ships built on the Pacific coast—to continue his journey around the world? Did part of his Pacific fleet reach Kaua'i, the northern most Hawaiian Island, thanks to the northeasterly trade winds? Possibly, but probably we will never know for sure. Legends persist however, of other people reaching Hawaii besides the Polynesians. The Nawao are said to have been a legendary people, an unknown, wild, large-sized hunting people, and the Menehune/Manahune (Tellem? or Pygmies?) are said to have been little people who built *heiau* (temples), ditch walls and fishponds of squared, smoothed and fitted basaltic stonework, perhaps similar to the mud or adobe blocks that were used for construction in the Mali Empire.

Walled temple (heiau) at Waimea, Kaua'i, from Captain Cook's third voyage, drawn by John Webber. Notice the difference in stone work between the irregular stones on the left (Polynesian?) and the faced and fitted ones on the right (Menehune?) public domain illustration

This suggests that there existed ancient peoples who settled the islands before the Polynesian descended Hawaiians reached the Menehune island of Kaua'i. "Legend states that the only foods available in Hawaii on the arrival of the Menehune were the fruit of the pandanus, the pith of the fern tree, the root of the *cordyline* and the berries of the *ohelo* and *akala*. In Kaua'I, the stronghold of the Menehune, there are two forms of stone pounders which are not found in any of the other islands of the group. They are termed 'ring pounders' and 'stirrup pounders' because of their shape, and they have comparatively narrow, elliptical pounding surfaces which form a marked contrast to the large, convex, rounded surfaces of the pounders used in the other islands to pound the taro tuber into the poi paste that formed the staple food of the later inhabitants."[101] As the Polynesian peoples expanded their settlements, the Menehune are said to have retreated into the mountain forests.

kauaikolea2 blog, posted the following on June 28, 2011:

> They enjoyed dancing, singing and archery, and their favorite foods were bananas and fish.... Menehune also enjoy cliff diving, and according to local lore, they were smart, extremely strong and excellent craftsmen. They were rarely seen by human eyes, and they are credited with mighty feats of engineering and overnight construction.

> These industrious master builders used their great strength to build temples (heiaus), fishponds, roads, canoes and houses. A few people believe they are responsible for the construction of some surprising structures in ancient Hawaii, including the 'Menehune ditch'—an aqua duct that funnels water for irrigation from the Waimea River on Kauai— and the legendary 'overnight' creation of the Alekoko fishpond on Kauai....

It is said that:

> Interrupted by the sun, the Menehune left two gaps in the fishpond wall. Many generations later, Chinese settlers filled the gaps to raise

mullet, but the stonework which closed the gap was far inferior to that of the mystical Menehune.

Even though the Menehune were said to be displaced when the first settlers arrived, some people still believe that the Menehune are roaming the islands, carrying out tricks on people. Indeed, an 1820 census of Kauai listed 65 people as "Menehune."[102]

There stands on the pali of Waikolu, near Kalaupapa, Molokai, a *heiau* (temple) that Hawaiians believe to have been constructed by no one else than the Menehunes. It is on the top of a ledge in the <u>face of a perpendicular cliff</u>, with a continuous inaccessible cliff behind it reaching hundreds of feet above. No one has ever been able to reach it either from above or from below; and the marvel is how the material, which appears to be seashore stones, was put in place.[103] Could this possibly suggest that the Menehune were actually the Tellem pygmies of the Bandiagara Escarpment in Mali, since the Tellem built their homes on <u>inaccessible cliff ledges</u> in that African escarpment?

Based on a photograph by Ann Thompson, a small thatched hut was supposedly discovered when "she came across this scene while hiking through a remote valley about three miles off the main Kalalau trail on Kauai. She claims to have seen 'a very small man, approximately 3 feet tall' near a small thatched hut. The 'pygmy-like' tribesman ran into the forest after he saw her. Ann says she heard other voices and bird whistle sounds, but did not go closer because she thought the man may have had a bow and arrows slung across his back."[104]

Stone Statues of Menehune in Hawaii. Notice the thick lips and protruding eyes. This is a public domain photograph.

An elderly docent (guide) at the Bishop Museum in Honolulu, Hawaii, told this author, as he interviewed her on February 9, 2018, that her father had claimed to have once seen a Menehune. Arthur Ribbel of the San Diego Union Tribune stated in 1986 that: "They (the Menehune) seem never at rest but are forever tumbling, doing handstands, juggling and forming themselves in circles and pyramids." Does this observation remind anyone of the Pottery Mound, New Mexico, kiva painting of the black tumbling figure? So the question is—did Abu Bakr II have little people with him?

Pygmies? Possibly since Fray Garcés thought he had seen *Chicos* (small or short people) at Hopi Pueblo in 1776.

That Abu Bakr II preceded the Spanish exploration of the American Southwest by over 200 years does not detract from the daring journeys of men like Cabeza de Vaca, Esteban the Moor, Fray Marcos de Niza, Vázquez de Coronado, Espejo, Oñate, de Anza, Fray Garcés and many others. Abu Bakr and the Spanish explorers were from different eras and had different goals. Christopher Columbus' achievement was equally as daring and significant as Abu Bakr II's, but completely separate. However, Columbus may have had personal knowledge of Atlantic width (about 5055 kilometers or 3141 miles from Dakar, Senegal to St. Thomas, Virgin Islands), currents and winds, and perhaps an indication that Cathay (China) was reachable, gained through experience on previous sailings (Bristol, England, to Iceland in 1477). Other information may have come from English sailors (Bristol merchants/sailors Thomas Croft, Robert Thorne and Hugh Eliot were claimed to have been the first Englishmen to sail across the Atlantic Ocean before Columbus). There also were knowledgeable informants like the Pinzón brothers, captains of La Pinta and La Niña, and Pedro Alonso Niño, Columbus' pilot[105] But there is no evidence that Columbus even knew of Abu Bakr II's tremendous accomplishment. On the other hand, Columbus never traveled inland far enough to find Texas, New Mexico, Arizona or the Californias. Perhaps Columbus also should have brought an elephant to ride across the Americas.

If you liked this history's mystery—wait until you read this author's next book titled *Mystery Mountain: Solving the Puzzle of the Los Lunas, New Mexico, Decalogue*.

Impact

The Emperor's voyage and exploration of the "unknown world" certainly made an impression on the Indians of the North American Southwest, even if it didn't make news in Europe or the United States.

It is fine to write about the first person from Africa to successfully explore the American Southwest (putting Esteban the Black [Moor, Slave] in second place, but one has to wonder what impact this mysterious explorer had on the Native Americans he encountered. Fortunately he and the local people left clues.

Archeologists have discovered that the Brownsville Complex of the lower Rio Grande Valley, between 1300 CE and 1400 CE, was trading shell beads for obsidian (a much desired natural cutting material) with the Huastec people of the Veracruz region. If those shells appeared as a result of trade for food with Abu Bakr II's flotilla, then there was a substantial economic impact resulting in improved tool and weapon technology for residents of the lower Rio Grande Valley. Obsidian (volcanic glass) can be utilized as sharp knife blades and scrapers as well as thinner edged spear points and arrow heads.

As Abu Bakr II's caravan moved closer to Pueblo land, the more opportunity there was for noticeable impact. At Pottery Mound ruin, south of present-day Albuquerque, New Mexico, the most noticeable impact may have been in its Painted Kiva, where in addition to providing a subject (twirling upside down black figure) of artistic interest, there may have been an entertainment element. Perhaps the Emperor's entourage included acrobats, tumblers and jugglers as well as praise singers—African style. This may have resulted in a social impact on the Pueblo people. In addition, "Pottery Mound is named after the large number of potsherds lying on the site surface, and after its low mound of melted adobe. The site was part of the Rio Grande Glaze Ware tradition that began circa 1315 CE and continued until the time of the Spanish re-conquest of New Mexico in 1693 CE. The site's signature pottery, Pottery Mound Polychrome, includes red and black paint on a background consisting of two slip colors (on bowls, one slip color on the inside and the other on the outside)" according to Wikipedia's, "Pottery Mound" article. Given the approximate date so close to Abu Bakr II's visit about 1312, one has to wonder if the impact of his visit contributed to the creation of this new style of pottery, or whether it was mere coincidence.

Determining religious impact is fairly easy if there are pictures. At Kuaua Pueblo ruin it is especially easy since the resident artist painted an excellent representation of a rain spirit on the below ground Painted Kiva wall. In this case the painting is clearly a goateed black figure holding an umbrella with thundercloud, lightning and rain in the background. The figure appears to be partially framed by an elephant tusk. It can be interpreted as Abu Bakr II's timely arrival at the beginning of an especially rainy monsoon season near the end of the prolonged drought that had forced some Pueblo peoples to relocate to the Rio Grande Valley. His timely arrival at Kuaua could have been enough of a coincidence to label him as a religious rain spirit, thus meriting a religious portrait along with "Sky Father", "Earth Mother", etc.

Cultural impact can consist of many types of influences. A Keres speaking community in New Mexico apparently chose to create a black *kachina* based on the Emperor's appearance. This *kachina* was eventually adopted by the Zuni and Hopi Pueblos who turned the *kachina* into an ogre figure to scare children when they tried to go outside the Pueblo, according to this author's informant. The impact of this Emperor was therefore to aid them in creating a "boogieman" cultural icon that was used as a *kachina*, ceremonial gourd rattling dancer and an impersonator whose task it was to keep children under control. The *kachinas*, which were named Chakwaina, contain copies of the Emperor's sea shell double bandolier, chin whiskers, gold skull cap crown and gold broad collar. The "uncle" figure has protruding eyes (as mentioned by the Diné (Navajos). The "nephew" figure has upside down crescent eyes. It is conceivable that the Emperor brought a nephew, as well as other relatives with him, resulting in two Chakwaina cultural figures.

This intrusion into Native American cultures by the Emperor's caravan had a significant impact on the early Diné (Navajo). This impact can be detected in the Navajo Black

World creation myth which probably would not exist without the Emperor's travel through "Dinétah" near the confluence of Cañon Largo and the San Juan River in Northwestern New Mexico. As the strange caravan approached the Navajo settlements in single file, the Navajo myth maker saw the strangers as black ant people with thick lips and protruding eyes (supporting *kachina* indicator). Therefore, the Emperor's visit profoundly affected the oral history and mythology of this people for centuries to come.

The elephant pitcher of Montezuma Valley is an example of the impact that the Emperor's elephants had on the design of some pottery. It would be interesting to know if other designs were influenced by African animals or patterns. The "Elephant Slabs" must have had a religious impact on the Flora Vista pueblo to have been safely hidden away in the carefully buried condition that they were, but it cannot be proved. Nevertheless, the Indians of Flora Vista Pueblo probably felt they were unique since written inscriptions were usually considered sacred.

Another impact could be described as geographical since it is concerned with the naming of a spring and watering hole by an Indian group, perhaps the Cochimi, in Baja California. The spring sports the same name as the Emperor's dynastic family name—KEITA—what a coincidence! Of course it is not by coincidence. The Indian group saw fit to name the spring for the Emperor's family because the Emperor's family and party occupied its site for an extended period of time while his scouts probably searched for the ideal Pacific harbor for constructing a new fleet.

The impacts that the Emperor's traveling party made on American natives have had a long lasting effect on hunter gatherers, Pueblo peoples, Navajos and geography. Other researchers of Indian history such as historians, geographers, anthropologists, archeologists and graduate students have a good chance to discover even further impacts.

Appendix 1: Education

Once there was an Emperor (Sultan, King-of-Kings) who was said to value exploration more than personal imperial power. His name was Abu Bakr II, or Abubakari II. He was the *Mansa* (King of Kings) of the West African Empire of Mali (composed of twelve kingdoms) bordering the Atlantic Ocean. He was VERY POWERFUL. Each king of the 12 kingdoms stabbed his spear into the ground before the imperial throne. Each king had thereby relinquished his kingdom to the Keita dynasty centered in Niani. Abu Bakr II was also VERY RICH since the emperor's treasury took possession of all gold from the mines which his great uncle had captured from the old Ghana Empire.

It is most likely that Bata Manding Bory Keita (later known as Abu Bakr II), the Imperial Prince, was tutored by Arabic teachers. His tutors might have included an Arabic geographer who showed the prince that the world was round like a gourd. The prince might also have had available to him a strong Middle-eastern tradition of astronomy and geometry with records of longitude from the Middle East revealing that in 1267 the Arab astronomer Zamaruddin built the first wooden global sphere with latitudes and longitudes and correct ratio sea/land of 70/30. Arab historian and geographer Al-Mas'udi knew that the world was round since he stated: *"If you sail on the sea, land and mountains disappear gradually, until you lose even the sight of highest summits of the mountains, and, on the contrary, if you approach the coast, you gradually perceive, first, the mountains, and, when you come nearer, you see the trees and plains".*[18]

This amazing global revelation probably fascinated the impressionable prince, who up until this time most likely thought that everything he had seen—desert, sahel and savanna—indicated that the world was flat. The Imperial family greatly benefited from contacts with the educated Islamic cultures. The knowledgeable teacher (like the 13th Century French geographer who stated that *"a man could go around the world, as a fly makes the tour of an apple"*) probably also emphasized that if one traveled around the world, <u>he would end up where he had started.</u> This idea of circumnavigating the world appears to have caught the fancy of the young prince, and dominated his thinking from that time forward. Perhaps he even had a chance to see and study a copy of Arab historian and geographer Al-Mas'udi's pre-956 world map on which "Ard Majhoola" or "unknown land" appears near "Sudan" (Africa) and the world appears to be surrounded by water. Notice how much his "Ard Majhoola" resembles the South American east coast, with an indentation where perhaps the Amazon River was known to be.

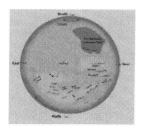

Pre-956 CE translated map of the world (oriented with South at the top) by the Arab historian and geographer Al-Mas'udi. The "unknown land" or "Ard Majhoola" may refer to the Americas. Public domain map.

Appendix 2: Culture and People of Abu Bakr II's Mali Empire

The *Encyclopedia Britannica* describes the Mandinka people of Mali as "a vigorous, well-proportioned, longheaded, big-jowled, flat-nosed people with projecting cheekbones and regular features". Malians are known to have frequently gathered for traditional festivals, dances, and ceremonies. Most Malians are said to have worn flowing, colorful robes called *boubous* that were typical of West Africa.

Mali people also might have covered themselves with fabric containing designs with specific meaning. Known as hand-painted mud cloth, also called *bogolan*[4,] it is one of Africa's most unusual and unique textiles. It consists of narrow strips of handwoven cotton which are stitched together into a whole cloth, then painted with patterns and symbols using a variety of natural dyes, including river mud that has been aged up to one year; usually, each cloth is a unique creation.

Fabrics like these represent an example of Mali clothes that some members of the Emperor's party, or even the Emperor himself, might have worn. They were made of natural materials and decorated using natural dyes. From these fabrics (materials, colors and designs) you can understand lots of things about the owner like his tribe or kingdom, social status and even if he is married.

Even the *jeliw* (plural) would have worn their clan designs in their clothing. The *jeli* (aka *griot* by the French) was a specialist in praise-music, singing and playing the usual, traditional ancestor and important person praise-songs. Some of the songs emphasized willingness of the people of Mali to lay down their lives for their emperor and nation. The Emperor, probably being a very vain person, would have thoroughly enjoyed his *jeliw*'s praises. He, of course, would have included his personal *jeliw* singers in his entourage. One can just imagine them playing and singing his praises each morning, noon and evening—whenever he descended from his imperial elephant's pavilion to eat or rest.

Griots de Sambala, roi de Médine (illustration de *Côte occidentale d'Afrique* du Colonel Frey) - Fig.81 p.128 - [Cote : Réserve A 200 386] 1890, source: Bibliothèque nationale de France, Jeanniot (grav.) This image from the National Library of France (BnF) is a reproduction by scanning of a bi-dimensional work that is now in the public domain. For this reason, it is in the public domain.

Jeliw (plural) were musicians/oral historians whose art and knowledge were transmitted from generation to generation within families. The *balafon* or *bala* [xylophone to which a gourd resonator is attached below each key] "is found from Mali to Guinea including Senegal, The Gambia, Guinea-Bissau, the Republic of Guinea, and Sierra Leone".[5] It is one of the oldest of the *jeli* instruments and oral accounts trace its origin at least as far back as the thirteenth century and the days of Abu Bakr II's great uncle Sunjata Keita, the founder and first ruler of the Mali Empire.[6]

Sculpture of jeliw/griots playing a *balafon* with big gourd resonators, http://tcd.freehosting.net/djembemande/bala.html; in the public domain.

A Bambara artist carving a *chi wara* headdress in the Bamako region of Mali. Photograph by Eliot Elisofon, 1971. Eliot Elisofon Photographic Archives (EEPA EECL 6751) National Museum of African Art, Smithsonian Institution; in the public domain.

Carving of wooden sculptures became a traditional, sacred, and artistic expression of Mali culture. The New Orleans African American Museum's "Bambara" website describes *chi wara* headdresses: *"*These headdresses feature the antelope, giving visual form to important religious beliefs about fertility and growth. They were worn in dances at the beginning of the rainy season (or when a fallow field was re-seeded) to assure a good harvest. Dancers who wore these headdresses covered their bodies with long grasses and cloth. They went bent over using two canes, believing that if they stood upright, they would offend the deity. The dancers accompanied farmers to the fields, supervised the planting, and then returned to the village where they danced. The dance consisted of jumps, sudden leaps and turns reminiscent of the actions of the antelope."

Although the dominant culture was called Mande, other people of various ethnic and linguistic traditions were present also. The Mande combined millet production with the rearing of livestock, but moved southwest from central Sahara as the latter became more unfit for agriculture and cattle-raising due to desertification. The Gambia, Senegal, Niger and smaller river valleys attracted these migrants. The various peoples developed into noble, merchant, artisan, blacksmith, military, praise-singer, slave, etc. classes. For instance most of the camel caravansaries were ethnic Tuareg nomads who lived in and around the Sahara Desert. They were camel transportation experts. The Emperor would have used them to import European and Middle Eastern goods for his rich court.

Postcard of a Tuareg displayed with his camel in the 1907 Colonial Exposition. French: Photographe anonyme (LL.): *Exposition Coloniale 1907. Touareg sur son Mehari.* carte postale nr 87, 1907. Unknown photographer. Picture is in the public domain.

Appendix 3: Mali Imperial Court

Let us try to understand what Abu Bakr II would have expected from his subjects by seeing what a *Mansa,* or King of 12 Kingdoms, was accustomed to in Mali—a gold rich empire located between Timbuktu/Niger River and the Atlantic coasts of present-day Senegal and The Gambia in Africa. Muslim traveler Ibn Battuta is our very knowledgeable guide.

(left) Ibn Battuta memorial plaque (in French) in Timbuktu, Mali; (right) Ibn Battuta traveled to Mali on "ships of the desert" like these. Public domain illustrations by Cresques Abraham on his 1375 Catalan Atlas.

Ibn Battuta's name in Arabic was: أبو عبد الله محمد بن عبد الله اللواتي الطنجي بن بطوطة, which was translated into English as *'Abū 'Abd al-Lāh Muḥammad ibn 'Abd al-Lāh l-Lawātī ṭ-Ṭanğī ibn Baṭūṭah.*[3] He was a famous thirty year traveler (from a Berber tribe known as the Lawata), who visited Mali in 1352. The following is what a Mali emperor was accustomed to doing, according to Ibn Battuta:

> On certain days the sultan holds audiences in
> the palace yard, where there is a platform

223

under a tree, with three steps; this they call the *pempi*. It is carpeted with silk and has cushions placed on it. [Over it] is raised the umbrella, which is a sort of pavilion made of silk, surmounted by a bird in gold, about the size of a falcon. The sultan comes out of a door in a corner of the palace, carrying a bow in his hand and a quiver on his back. On his head he has a golden skull-cap, bound with a gold band which has narrow ends shaped like knives, more than a span in length. His usual dress is a velvety red tunic, made of the European fabrics called *mutanfas*. The sultan is preceded by his musicians, who carry gold and silver *guimbris* [two-stringed guitars], and behind him come three hundred armed slaves. He walks in a leisurely fashion, affecting a very slow movement, and even stops from time to time. On reaching the *pempi* he stops and looks round the assembly, then ascends it in the sedate manner of a preacher ascending a mosque-pulpit. As he takes his seat the drums, trumpets, and bugles are sounded. Three slaves go out at a run to summon the sovereign's deputy and the military commanders, who enter and sit down. Two saddled and bridled horses are brought, along with two goats, which they hold to serve as a protection against the evil eye....

Emperor of Mali (1312-1337) holding a golden coin or nugget from Wikipedia, "Musa I of Mali"; originally on *Catalan Atlas,* 1375, produced by the Majorcan cartographic school and attributed to Cresques Abraham (also known as "Abraham Cresques"), a Jewish book illuminator. This map image is in the public domain.

225

Ibn Battuta, the famous 14th century traveler, continued to observe that:

> The [Blacks] are of all people the most submissive to their king and the most abject in their behavior before him. They swear by his name, saying "Mansa {name} ki" [in Mandinka], "the Emperor {his name} has commanded" [in English]. If he summons any of them while he is holding an audience in his pavilion, the person summoned takes off his clothes and puts on worn garments, removes his turban and dons a dirty skullcap, and enters with his garments and trousers raised knee-high. He goes forward in an attitude of humility and dejection and knocks the ground hard with his elbows, then stands with bowed head and bent back listening to what he says. If anyone addresses the king and receives a reply from him, he uncovers his back and throws dust over his head and back, for all the world like a bather splashing himself with water.... The armour-bearers bring in magnificent arms—quivers of gold and silver, swords ornamented with gold and with golden scabbards, gold and silver lances, and crystal maces. The women servants, slave-girls, and young girls go about in front of everyone naked, without a stitch of clothing on them. Women go into the sultan's presence naked

and without coverings, and his daughters also go about naked.[3]

Similar to Mali's King-of-Kings, Agnibilécro - Kangan, Chef Agnis holds court for the postcard photographer G. Kante, circa 1920. "The seated ruler wears a *Bondoukou* style cloth which represents an important stylistic and historical link between the textiles of Mali ... and those of Ghana" from http://adireafricantextiles.blogspot.co.uk/2013/08/revisiting-some-exceptional-bondoukou.html. In the public domain. The original postcard is in the Museum of Fine Arts, Boston, Leonard A. Lauder Postcard Archive—Gift of Leonard A. Lauder. Accession no. 2012.5386.

Appendix 4: Abu Bakr II's Decision to Explore

T. S. Eliot possibly summed up Abu Bakr II's thoughts best when he wrote in his poem *Little Gidding* that "We shall not cease from exploration and the end of all our exploring will be to arrive where we began...."

How do we know Abu Bakr II's decision? His successor revealed the whole process of Abu Bakr II's growing resolve:

In *"Masalik as absar fi mamulite al-amsar"* (kept in the Ahmet III Library in Istanbul), edited and translated by Gaudefroy-Demombynes in *L'Afrique Moins l'Egypt"*, Paris, 1927, Arab-Egyptian scholar *Shihāb ad-Dīn Aḥmad ibn Faḍl Allāh al-'Umarī* (شهاب الدين أبو العبّاس أحمد بن فضل الله الـ عمري) (known in the West as Al-Umari)[7] reported a story told to Ibn Amir Hajib, governor of Cairo, in 1324, by Abu Bakr II's successor, Mali *Mansa* (King of Kings) Musa, who went on a pilgrimage (*Al Hajj*) to Mecca.

Musa's "procession reportedly included 60,000 men, including 12,000 slaves who each carried four pounds of gold bars, organized horses, and handled bags. Musa provided all necessities for the procession, feeding the entire company of men and animals."[8] Those animals included 80 camels which each carried between 50 and 300 pounds of gold dust.

Musa gave gold to the poor he met along his route. He not only gave gold to the cities he passed on the way to Mecca, including Cairo and Medina, but also traded gold for souvenirs. Musa wanted to impress the Arab world with Mali's wealth in order to attract scholars, architects and other

A 13th-century book illustration produced in Baghdad by al-Wasiti showing a group of pilgrims on a *hajj*—note the camels. This painting is from a manuscript of *Maqâmât* of al-Harîrî; Yahyâ ibn Mahmûd al-Wâsitî - The Yorck Project: *10.000 Meisterwerke der Malerei;* from Wikipedia Commons. This image is in the public domain.

specialists, but distributed so much gold that it ruined the Egyptian economy for at least twelve years, according to Ibn Battuta. Mansa Musa's pilgrimage boosted Islamic education in Mali by adding mosques, libraries, and universities. The awareness of Musa by other Islamic leaders brought increased commerce and scholars, poets, and artisans, making Timbuktu one of the leading cities in the Islamic world. Timbuktu with its famous university and busy market place was clearly the center of Islamic Sub-Saharan Africa.

Postcard of the market place, *La Place du Marché*, Timbuktu, Western Africa (Mali), circa 1925. Unknown photographer. Public domain picture.

I asked the Sultan Musa, says Ibn Amir Hajib, how it was that power came into his [Musa's] hands. We are he told me [Hajib] from a house that transmits power by heritage. The ruler [Abu Bakr II] who preceded me would not believe that it was impossible to discover the limits of the neighboring sea. He wanted to find out and persisted in his plan. He had two hundred ships equipped and filled with men, and others in the same number filled with gold, water, and supplies in sufficient quantity to last for years; [supplies that they would need, not only to cross the dangerous ocean, but to explore the other side]. He told those who commanded them: "Return only when you have reached the extremity of the ocean, or when you have exhausted your food and water." They went away, their absence was long, before any of them returned. Finally, a sole ship reappeared. We asked the captain about their adventures. "Prince", he replied, "We sailed a long time, up to the moment when we encountered in mid-ocean something like a river with a violent current [possibly the Canaries, North Equatorial or Antilles Current from about 7°N to about 20°N]. My ship was last. The others sailed on, and gradually as each one entered the place, they disappeared and did not come back.

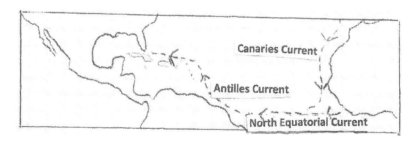

Major Atlantic Ocean Currents: Canaries, North Equatorial and Antilles. Map created by Ronald Stewart.

Another version states that perhaps "they were drowned in the great whirlpool and never came out again."[9]

Ocean whirlpools, or maelstroms, are real! This mysterious whirlpool was spotted in the Atlantic Ocean; photograph is in the public domain.

Emperor Musa continued telling the returned ship captain's story and his own assumption of power as "Master of the Empire" The sole surviving captain revealed that:

> We did not know what had happened to them.
> As for me, I returned to where I was and did
> not enter the current.

Musa added: *"But the emperor did not want to believe him."*

Frantz Fanon stated in *Black Skin, White Masks,* 1952: "Sometimes people hold a core belief that is very strong. When they are presented with evidence that works against that belief, the new evidence cannot be accepted. It would create a feeling that is extremely uncomfortable, called cognitive dissonance. And because it is so important to protect the core belief, they will rationalize, ignore and even deny anything that doesn't fit in with the core belief." This may explain why Abu Bakr II couldn't accept the truth. Musa continued his story:

> The Emperor [Abu Bakr II] was so intrigued by this Captain's news that he became determined to follow up. He equipped two thousand vessels, a thousand for himself and the men who accompanied him and a thousand for water and supplies. He conferred power [and the regency] on me [Musa] for the term of his absence and left with his companions on the ocean. This was the last time that I saw him and the others, and I remained the absolute master of the empire.[9]

A different scenario concerning the first expedition has been suggested. Is it possible that the one ship that returned was the designated messenger to report to the Emperor the successful trans-Atlantic voyage of the others, and therefore the sailors were ordered by *Mansa* Abu Bakr II to give disinformation to the public to discourage other possible adventurers? Dr. Muhammad Hamidullah has surmised that: "...apparently the ruler did not want the news of the discovery of America to reach his rivals. So he caused the captain to tell discouraging things in public and real facts in private."[9] This practice of disinformation was not uncommon for paranoiac rulers.

Also, according to Malian scholar Gaoussou Diawara in his book, *The Saga of Abubakari II...* "he [Abu Bakr II] left with 2000 boats, the emperor gave up all power and gold to pursue knowledge and discovery. Abubakari's ambition was to explore whether the Atlantic Ocean—like the great River Niger that swept through Mali—had another 'bank'. In 1311 [710-711 Islamic calendar], he handed the throne over to his relative, *Kankan* [deputy] Moussa, and set off on an expedition into the unknown."[10] Mark Hyman filled in some of the details by saying that: "Abu Bakr II was interested in scholars' stories of a "gourd-shaped world, the big ocean to the west [Atlantic Ocean] and the new world beyond that". Hyman claims that the *Mansa* interviewed sail-builders from Egypt and Mediterranean cities, gathered shipbuilders and watermen from all over his empire and decided to build ships on the coast of Sene-Gambia, between the Gambia and Senegal Rivers. "The silk cotton tree provided many of the most suitable logs for massive canoe building, and launching was via wooden rollers to the water. Boat building specialists were to emerge among certain tribes, particularly in the Niger Delta."[11]

Appendix 5: Mali Ship Building Technology

Shipbuilding. Wikimedia Commons, Public domain.

Abu Bakr II is said to have had different boat designs built so that if one failed another might succeed. Apparently there was an abundant supply of wood in the Sene-Gambia region with which to build large ships. They were usually carved from a single silk cotton tree trunk which was used as the backbone. Planks were then fitted alongside to enlarge them. Cabins were built on top of the interior out of woven mat or other strong fibrous material.

Dr. Peregrino Brimah relates a story about the Sorko people:

"Sorko, Lords of the Sea

The Sorko dug out canoes by hollowing out
trunks of trees.
Drilling holes in planks and binding them
together, they made the Kanta, larger ships
strong enough to conquer the seas.
The Sorko capital was Kebbi in today's
Nigeria; it was there they laid down the keel.
Bound tight with twine and leather strips,
holes were plugged with the burgu plant seal.
From Kebbi, Kanta were built and brought up
the river to Gao, the Songhai capital.
The Sorko, masters of the sea were ready to
go intercontinental.
With these great ships did the indomitable
Songhai set sail.
The new land, the Americas, the adventurers
of Timbuktu did unveil." [12]

In *Fishing for Development: Small-scale fisheries in Africa,*
Inge Tvedten and Bjørn Hersoug, eds. 1992, stated that "The
Songhai 'kanta' [large boat] could carry up to 30 tons of
goods, i.e. the load capacity of 1000 men, 200 camels, 300
cattle or a flotilla of 20 regular canoes."[12] Some of these
boats had an even greater load capacity of 50 to 80 tons. Yes,
Africans could build large enough ships to sail across the
Atlantic—even large enough to transport camels and
elephants! Europeans and Americans have continually

underestimated the knowledge and skills of some African peoples.

Two eighteenth century European observers noted the presence of large fleets along this [Atlantic] coast. Both Jean Barbot *(A Description of the Coasts of North and South-Guinea*, 1732) and Anthony Benezet (*Some Historical Account of Guinea*, 1772) reported that as many as 800 canoes left the Gold Coast [modern Ghana] daily on fishing expeditions.

The Atlantic fishermen and island traders had known how to build and sail large dugout wooden ships for eons. They utilized the giant silk cotton tree that grew along the Atlantic coastline between The Senegal and The Gambia Rivers, among others. They then built up the sides of their dugouts with sewn and caulked planks. These proved to be very seaworthy.

Dufuna Canoe "Africa's oldest known boat" (circa 6,000 BCE) discovered in 1987, proving that West Africans were aware of sophisticated pointed-prow technology in ancient times. Public domain.

"The civilization of Africa developed very sophisticated vessels. They built reed boats with and without sails, log rafts lashed together, dugouts as wide-berthed Viking[like] ships, double-canoes, lateen-rigged dhows, jointed boats, and rope sewn plank vessels with straw cabins and cooking facilities,... carrying cargo from food and people, to <u>elephants</u> [underlined by this author] and building material."[13]

> Some canoes were 80 feet (24 m) in length, carrying 100 men or more. Documents from 1506 for example, refer to war-canoes on the Sierra Leone river, carrying 120 men. Others refer to Guinea coast peoples using canoes of varying sizes—some 70 feet (21 m) in length, 7–8 ft. broad, with sharp pointed ends, rowing benches on the side, and quarter decks or focastles [forecastle, raised front of a ship] build of reeds, and miscellaneous facilities such as cooking hearths, and storage spaces for crew sleeping mats. These boats were usually six to eight feet across and about fifty feet long. There is evidence that Emperor Abu Bakar II of Mali used these "*almadias*" or longboats.[14]

Cargo laden boat on the Niger River on an Afrique Occidentale Française stamp.

Large capacity pirogues on a Senegalese stamp. These stamps are in the public domain.

Appendix 6: Survivalists

In 1952, Dr. Alain Bombard (October 27, 1924 – July 19, 2005) sailed from Casablanca to Barbados in a small boat he named *L'Heretique*, developing survival techniques along the way. In *The Bombard Story*, he stated: *"I claim to have proved that the sea itself provides sufficient food and drink to enable the battle for survival to be fought with perfect confidence."*

Hannes Lindeman (28 December 1922 - 17 April 2015), also a doctor, stated in his 1958 book, *Alone At Sea*, that he himself decided to study the problems of survival at sea in a native <u>African</u> <u>dugout</u> <u>canoe</u> in the 1950s. The inquisitive doctor sailed a second-hand 23 foot mahogany tree dugout across the Atlantic in 65 days, seeing cormorant, shearwater and petrel birds dance over the waves, and red-billed tropic birds (Linnaeus' son-of-the-sun) which flew over his dugout. They sported long tail feathers, with a salmon red touch on their wings, a lobster-colored beak, a black band near their eyes and black stripes on their wings— easily distinguishable markings. They were the same size as gulls but unlike them they flew high above the water's surface, flapping their wings with untiring energy. Then there were pilot fish, sharks, bioluminescent plankton, water striders, whales and Portuguese men-of-war. Flying fish leaped into the air. He speared and feasted on dolphins, ate barnacles, which clung to the dugout, and triggerfish which also found barnacles edible. In the soft light of early morning one day, he finally saw frigate birds which he knew were seldom seen more than one hundred miles offshore. He arrived in the Virgin Islands after 65 days of becalming and stormy weathers. Doctor

Lindeman concluded by saying *"My adventurous voyage had proved that primitive vessels, although unable to sail against the wind, can not only cross the ocean but can reach their goal. Was mine the first African canoe ever to touch American soil? I doubt it."*

Most European sailors and navigators concluded that sailors undertaking a westward voyage from Europe to Asia non-stop would die of <u>thirst, scurvy</u> or <u>starvation</u> long before reaching their destination. This was only true for those who were ill-prepared. Casks of water, no matter how putrid it became, were essential in an ocean composed of seawater (3.5% salinity). The sailors' predicament was perfectly described by a line in Samuel Taylor Coleridge's *The Rime of the Ancient Mariner*: *Water, water, everywhere, nor any drop to drink."* According to Thor Heyerdahl, when mixed with fresh water in a 2:3 ratio, however, seawater seems to have no ill effects for humans. Starvation, it also appears, can be avoided by being willing to catch and consume whatever lives in the sea.

Christopher Columbus sailed from the Canary Islands to the Bahamas in five weeks, or 61 days total from Spain in 1492 CE. In 1970 CE, Thor Heyerdahl (October 6, 1914 – April 18, 2002) and crew finally succeeded in sailing a reed boat from Morocco to Barbados in 58 days. The reeds came from the African nation of Chad, just east of Mali. It is therefore assumed that Abu Bakr II's fleet probably took two to three months to cross from the Senegal River ports.

Barbados stamp picturing Ra II in the Atlantic Ocean nearing Barbados. This stamp is in the public domain.

Not all Mali ships were rudderless dugout canoes or reed boats like Ra II. However, those containing people would have had steering oars or rudders.

Ships with large rudders as depicted on modern Republic of Mali stamps. These stamps are in the public domain.

Rudders had to be large and strong. Dr. Lindeman found out the hard way how strongly they had to be attached to his craft. He broke two of them and had a shark bite through the rudder cable on the attempted trips in his dugout. Most likely some of the Emperor's ships had to be repaired at sea too, thus the need for ship carpenters and sturdy parts.

Appendix 7: What Lies Beyond The Sea of Fogs

Duarte Pacheco Pereira (15th century Portuguese) stated that West Africans "fished up to 100 leagues (circa 300/350 miles)" from the closest shores and it thus appears that they were mainly from Senegal (from Senegal to the Cape Verde Islands is 300/350 miles). Fishermen and sailors from the Mali Empire therefore probably knew the Eastern Atlantic waters and had ocean going vessels.

The Emperor's watery journey westward was <u>not</u> impossible. A few Muslim explorers previously had returned from their voyages west.[18] In *Muruj adh-Dhahab wa Ma'adin al-Jawhar*, volume 1, page 138 (The Meadows of Gold and Mines of Jewels) written around the year 956 CE [Common Era or A.D.], Abul Hassan Ali ibn al-Hussain ibn Ali al-Masudi, a historian, geographer, philosopher, and natural scientist, wrote about a young navigator of Cordoba named Khashkhash ibn Saeed ibn Aswad who collected a group of young men, crossed the Atlantic Ocean, made contact with people on the other side in a large area in the ocean of darkness and fog, [possibly called the "unknown territory" (*Ard Majhoola*) on al-Masudi's map][19], and returned in the year 889 CE with fabulous treasures. "Every Spaniard [Andalusian] knows his story." Al Masudi wrote: "Some people feel that this ocean is the source of all oceans and in it there have been many strange happenings. We have reported some of them in our book *Akhbar az-Zaman*. Adventurers have penetrated it at the risk of their lives, some returning safely, others perishing in the attempt," as reported on History of Islam website, "The African, and Muslim, Discovery of America—Before Columbus" by Dr. Abdullah Hakim Quick. These Muslim sailors sailed out of Delba (later known as Palos de la Frontera, Spain—Columbus' port) in an attempt to circle the globe. The ships were met by a great extent of land and native people with whom they traded before returning to Muslim Andalusia.

Another Muslim historian, Abu Bakr ibn Umar al-Qutiyya (not to be confused with the author of *Tarikh Iftitah al-Andalus*, Ibn al-Qutiyya) "narrated that during the reign of the Muslim caliph of Spain, Hisham II (976-1009 CE), another Muslim navigator, Ibn Farrukh, from Granada, sailed from Kadesh (February 999 CE) into the Atlantic, landed in Gando (Great Canary islands) visiting King Guanariga, and continued westward where he saw and named two islands, Capraria and Pluitana. He arrived back in Spain in May 999 CE"

"Abu Abd Allah Muhammad al-Idrisi al-Qurtubi al-Hasani al-Sabti, or simply Al Idrisi (Arabic: و أب بد ع الله محمد سي الإدري ي قرط ال الحسني تي ب س ال) (1090-1180), the famous Arab physician and geographer who established himself in the Arabicised court of King Roger II of Sicily, reported in his geographical work *Nuzhat al-Mushtaq* in the 12th century on the journey of a group of seamen who reached some Atlantic isles (perhaps only the Canary or Madeira Islands, but perhaps in the Americas,). Al Idrisi wrote:"

> Beyond this ocean of fogs it is not known
> what exists there. Nobody has the sure

knowledge of it, because it is very difficult to traverse it. Its atmosphere is foggy, its waves are very strong, its dangers are perilous, its beasts are terrible, and its winds are full of tempests. There are many islands, some of which are inhabited, others are submerged. No navigator traverses them but bypasses them remaining near their coast.... And it was from the town of Lisbon that the adventurers set out known under the name of *Mugharrarin* [Adventurers or Seduced Ones], penetrated the ocean of fogs and wanted to know what it contained and where it ended.... After sailing for twelve more days they perceived an island that seemed to be inhabited, and there were cultivated fields. They sailed that way to see what it contained. But soon barques encircled them and made them prisoners, and transported them to a miserable hamlet situated on the coast. There they landed. The navigators saw there people with red skin; there was not much hair on their body, the hair of their head was straight, and they were of high stature. Their women were of an extraordinary beauty.[20]

Same source, but a different version appeared on the Muslim Heritage website, Echos of What Lies Behind the "Ocean of Fogs" in Muslim Historical Narratives:

And it was from the town of Lisbon that the adventurers set out known under the name of

Mugharrarin (seduced ones), penetrated the ocean of fogs (Atlantic) and wanted to know what it contained and where it ended. In the town of Lisbon there is still near al-Hamma (source of thermal water, maybe modern Estoril), a street called *Darb al-mugharrarin ila akhir al-abad* (street of those seduced till the eternity). In fact eight persons, all cousins, prepared a boat of mercantile transport, filled it with water and victuals sufficing them for several months, then set sail. When the winds from the east began to blow, they profited by it to voyage for eleven days. They reached a part of the ocean with strong waves, ill smelling water, numerous shallow places and bad visibility [Sargasso Sea?]. Sure of perishing there, they turned the sails in another direction, and sailed towards the south for twelve days. They arrived then in face of the island of goats. In fact there were herds of goats, countless in number, pasturing freely without anyone herding them. The sailors went to the island and landed. There they found a source of water near which was a tree of wild fig. They captured some of the goats and slaughtered them, but found that the meat was so bitter that nobody could swallow it. So they kept only the skins and departed again, the southern wind pushing them. After sailing for twelve more days they perceived an island that seemed to be inhabited, and there were cultivated fields. They sailed that way to see what it contained. But soon barks encircled them and made them prisoners, and transported them to a miserable hamlet situated on the coast. There they landed. The navigators saw there *people with red skin*; there was not much hair on their body, the hair of their head was straight, and they were of high stature. Their women were of an extraordinary beauty. The navigators were shut in a house of the village for three days. On the fourth day somebody came to them who talked Arabic. He asked them who they were and why had they come. They gave all necessary information. The inquirer promised everything good, and told them that he was the interpreter of the king. The day following this inquiry, they were led before the king, who put to them the same questions and they gave the same answers, telling him that they had undertaken the adventure in the ocean to know what new and curious thing there was and also to ascertain where it ended. When the king heard that, he told the interpreter to inform them; 'My father had also commanded a group of slaves to navigate on this ocean, who did that for one whole month until they reached a place where there was no more light; they returned without seeing anything curious or obtaining any advantage.' Then the king told them through the interpreter that they need not fear, and that they could expect from the king nothing but good. Then they returned to their house-prison and remained there until the west breeze began to blow. Then the aborigines prepared a boat, blindfolded the navigators and sailed for a certain lapse of time. These unlucky (Muslims) supposed that they might have sailed for three days. Then they landed, and transported us, with hands tied behind our backs, and left us on the coast. We remained there till we felt the growing light of the rising sun. We were in a pitiable state. At last we heard sounds of men. We cried, and people came to us and found us wounded by the ropes tying us. They interrogated us. We gave them all the information they desired. These were Berbers. One of them asked us; 'Do you know how far you are from your country?' We said: 'No.' He continued: 'From here to your country there is a distance of two months [by camel caravan?].' The leader of the navigators exclaimed: '*Wa Asafi* (woe be to me!).' The region took this name and is still called Asafi. It is a port, as we have mentioned, in the extremity of Morocco.[17]

Muslim reference books mentioned a well-documented description of a journey across the sea of fog and darkness by Shaikh Zayn Eddine Ali Ben Fadhel Al-Mazandarani. His journey started from Tarfaya (South Morocco) during the reign of the King Abu-Yacoub Sidi Youssef (1286-1307 CE)

6th of the Marinid dynasty, to Green Island in the Caribbean sea in 1291 CE (690 HE).[18]

Of course, Vikings (Norse from Scandinavia) are known to have created a settlement at L'Anse aux Meadows, Newfoundland, Canada, but how many other adventurous European, African and Muslim sea traders accomplished these nautical feats is unknown. However, Columbus, Balboa and other Spanish explorers found people, cloth, gold tipped spears and other trade goods of African origin along the Atlantic coast and islands of the Americas. In 1498, Columbus recorded seeing a ship loaded with goods, heading towards America, filled with Africans who were probably on their way to trade with Native Americans. Columbus also records in his journal that Native Americans told him of black Africans who came regularly to trade with them.

Appendix 8: Preparations

Mark Hyman states that preparations for the journey included carpenters, smiths, navigators, merchants, potters, jewelers, weavers, magicians, diviners, thinkers, and the Mandinka military, and that every vessel tugged a supply-boat with food for two years, dried meat, grain, preserved fruit in ceramic jars, and gold for trade. Hyman also claims that key ships would communicate with drummers, using a *n'taman* [talking drum], and that all communications were coordinated from the leading ship of the fleet.[15]

The "talking drum" is an hourglass-shaped drum unique to West Africa, whose pitch can be regulated to mimic the tone and prosody (intonation & rhythm) of human speech It has two drumheads connected by leather tension cords which allow the player to modulate the pitch of the drum by squeezing the cords between his or her arm and body.

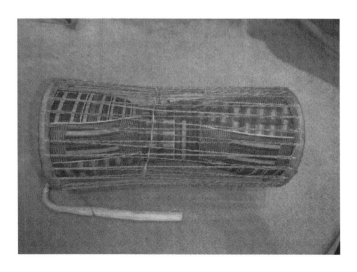

(above and previous) An authentic talking drum, made in Ghana, seen in the Maxwell Museum of Anthropology store, University of New Mexico, Albuquerque, New Mexico; now in the Ronald Stewart collection. Photographs courtesy of Joanne Stewart.

Man demonstrating how the talking drum [*tama*] is used. Found on babathestoryteller.com, which also demonstrates the use of string *kora*. Note the gentleman's goatee or chin whiskers. Public domain.

Appendix 9: Oral Historians

"… the scholars say the best sources of information on Abubakari II are *Griots*—the original historians in Africa. Mr. Diawara states that the paradox of Abubakari II, is that the *Griots* [Jeliw] themselves, imposed a long lasting seal of silence on the story. Traditionally, "negative *fadenya* can … signal an individual's complete break from society, in which one leaves and never returns with anything to benefit one's own family and people. This also brings about great shame."[16] "The *Griots* found his abdication a shameful act, not worthy of praise," Mr. Diawara said. "For that reason they have refused to sing praise or talk of this great African man."[16] However, Mr. Diawara also says that the *Griots* in West Africa such as Sadio Diabate, are slowly starting to divulge the secrets on Abubakari II.[17]

Griots (Jeliw) still exist today. West African griots at the New York City Griot Summit on November 26-28, 2012 at the Wave Hill Gardens overlooking the Hudson, in the Bronx. Photograph from http://splintersandcandy.com/ny-west-african-griot-summit-112612-112812, in the public domain.

Griots hold the memory of West Africa [and also play the 21 string *kora*]. At the festival marking the installation of a regional chief in Faraba Banta in October 1991, *griotte* Adama Suso sings and Ma Lamini Jobareth plays the *kora*. Also see Thomas A. Hale, *Griots and Griottes,* Indiana University Press, 1998. Photograph courtesy of Richard K. Priebe, Ph.D. Professor Emeritus, Virginia Commonwealth University.

"We are vessels of speech, we are the repositories which harbor secrets many centuries old ... without us the names of kings would vanish from [into] oblivion, we are the memory of mankind; by the spoken word we bring to life the deeds and exploits of kings for younger generations. History holds no mystery for us; we teach to the vulgar just as much as we want to teach them, for it is we who keep the keys to the twelve doors of Mali.... I teach the kings of their ancestors so that the lives of the ancients might serve them as an example, for the world is old but the future springs from the past."[106]

END NOTES

1. Joseph P. Sánchez, *Comparative Colonialism, the Spanish Black Legend and Spain's Legacy in the United States: Perspectives on American Latino Heritage and Our National Story*, Spanish Colonial Research Center, Albuquerque, N.M. National Park Service, 2013.

2. "Pre-Columbian trans-oceanic contact theories", Wikipedia, citing: Morison, Samuel Eliot (1963). *Journals & Other Documents on the Life & Voyages of Christopher Columbus*. New York: The Heritage Press. Pp. 262, 263; and Thacher, John Boyd (1903). *Christopher Columbus: his life, his work, his remains, as revealed by original printed and manuscript records, together with an essay on Peter Martyr of Anghera and Bartolomé De Las Casas, the first Historians of America*. New York: G. P. Putnam's Sons. pp. 379, 380.

3. Ibn Battuta, The full title of the manuscript تـ حـ فة الأ سـ فار وعجائـ ب الأمـ صار غرائـ ب فـ ي الـ نظار may be translated as *A Gift to Those Who Contemplate the Wonders of Cities and the Marvels of Travelling* or the *Rihla* الرحلة, *The Journey,* Chapter Twelve: Journey to West Africa (1351 – 1353) pp. 323-335. Shams ad-Din Abu Abd Allah Muhammad ibn Muhammad ibn Ibrahim al-at-Tanyi Luwati (in Arabic : شمس الـ ديـ ن أبـ و عـ بد الله محمد بـ ن محمد بـ ن راهيم إبـ الـ طـ نجي الـ لواتـ ي), better known as Ibn Battuta (ابـ ن بـ طوطة), was a traveler and explorer, born in Tangier

255

on 17 Rajab of the year 703 of the Hegira , corresponding to February 25 of 1304 CE, and died in 1368 or 1369 CE.

4. Mud Cloth/Bogolan, "Genuine hand-painted mud cloth from Mali", http://www.africanfabric.co.uk/fabrics-textiles/large-textiles-cloths/mud-cloth-bogolan.

5. Lynne Jessup, *Mandinka Balafon*, p. 19.

6. "Djembe & Mande Music Page", http://tcd.freehosting.net/djembemande/bala.html.

7. Shihāb al-Dīn Abū al-'Abbās Aḥmad b. Faḍl Allāh al-'Umarī (شهاب ن الـ دين و أبـ العبّاس أحمد ن بـ ضل ف الله الـ عمري), or simply al-'Umarī, (1300 – 1349) was an Arab historian, born in Damascus. Born as a scion of a family of bureaucrats, al-'Umarī (as his name implies), traced his origin to 'Umar, the second Islamic caliph. His father held the important post of kātib as-sirr (head of the chancery) of the Mamlūk Empire. During his life, his scholarly works and writings were used in the administration of the Mamlūk Empire's dominions of Egypt and Syria, and later became standard sources for Mamlūk history.

8. Wikipedia, "Musa I of Mali" from Goodwin, A.J.H. (1957), "The Medieval Empire of Ghana", *South African Archaeological Bulletin*, 12: 108–112, JSTOR 3886971; "Echos of What Lies Behind the 'Ocean of Fogs' in Muslim Historical Narratives". *Muslimheritage.com.* Retrieved 27 June 2015; and "Abbas Hamdani, An Islamic Background to the Voyages of Discovery,

Language and Literature" in *The Legacy of Muslim Spain* (Studien Und Texte Zur Geistesgeschichte Des Mittelalters), 1994, ed. Salma Khadra Jayyusi.

9. Henry Louis Gates, Jr., *100 Amazing Facts About the Negro,* New York: Pantheon Books, 2017, p. 184; https://www.thevintagenews.com/2016/06/15/meet-wealthiest-person-times-mansa-musa-c-1280-c-1337/; Dr. Abdullah Hakim Quick, "The African and Muslim Discovery of America—Before Columbus" from http://www.historyofislam.com.

10. Clyde Winters quoting M. Hamidullah, "Muslim Discovery of America before Columbus," *al-Ittihad*, vol. 4, no.2, (Mar., 68, p. 9).

11. Wikipedia, "History of science and technology in Africa" citing Robert Smith, "The Canoe in West African History", *The Journal of African History*, Vol. 11, No. 4 (1970), pp. 515–533.

12. Dr. Peregrino Brimah, *KADUNAVOICE THE VOICE OF A GREAT PEOPLE*, "Mungo Park Did Not Discover River Niger … but Mansa Abubakari II discovered America", August 12, 2013.

13. Raymond Mauny, (1961), *Tableau géographique de l'ouest africain au moyen age* (in French), Dakar: Institut français d'Afrique Noire, OCLC 6799191.

14. "Before Columbus, The Moors Were In America", Rasta Livewire blog. They Came Before Columbus, Ivan Van Sertima; Random House: 1975.

15. African Knowledge.com.

16. Wikipedia, "Fadenya".

17. BBC NEWS website, "Africa's 'greatest explorer" by Joan Baxter in Mali.

18. Wafin: Moroccan Connections in Ameica website, "Moroccans discovering America", by Amhal.

19. El-Mas'udi, (in Arabic): مروج الذهب ومعادن الجوهر (transliteration): *Muruj adh-dhahab wa ma'adin al-jawahir* (in English): *Historical Encyclopedia entitled Meadows of Gold and Mines of Gems*, translated from the Arabic by Aloys Sprenger, M.D., vol. 1. London: Oriental Translation Fund, MDCCCXLI, p. 211.

20. Wikipedia, Muhammed al-Idrisi.

21. Ivan Van Sertima, *Early America Revisited,* London: Transaction Publishers, 1998, Page 17.

22. Mohammed Hamidullah, "Muslim Discovery of America before Columbus", *Journal of the Muslim Students' Association of the United States and Canada* (Winter 1968). 4 (2): 7–9 [1] and http://www.muslimheritage.com/article/echos-what-lies-behind-ocean-fogs-muslim-historical-narratives.

23. Edited version of the article originally written by the late Professor Mohammed Hamidullah, "Muslim Discovery of America before Columbus", *Journal of the Muslim Students' Association of the United States and Canada.*

24. John Duffy, The Passage to the Colonies", Mississippi Valley Historical Review, 38 (1951), p.23.

25. A.C. Trowbridge, "Tertiary and Quaternary Geology of the Lower Rio Grande Region, Texas", Bulletin 837, United States Government Printing Office Washington: 1932, p. 15

26. Wikipedia, "Alvise Cadamosto".

27. See Dr. Douglas Richmond of the University of Texas at Arlington, Texas Black History Preservation Project website who wrote in "The Emergence of Afro-Tejano Society during the Spanish Colonial Period in Texas, 1528-1700", that ". . . Hispanic explorers encountered Africans at the mouth of the Rio Grande", who were believed to have been shipwrecked.

28. Dr. Clyde Winters Blog, "Ancient African Writing Systems and Knowledge", May 24, 2015.

29. The University of Texas, Institute of Texan Cultures at San Antonio; and Lyman D. Platt, Ph.D. "The Escandón Settlement of Nueva España", p. 3; islandmix – All Islands, All People" website thread: Mali Discovers America: before Columbus" quoting from the "Fanciful meeting of explorers and Native Americans, Institute of Texan Cultures, 84-77", 2000.

30. "All About Bison", https://allaboutbison.com/.

31. Jennifer L. Logan, "Chapter Nine. *Reassessing Cultural Extinction: Change and Survival at Mission San Juan Capistrano, Texas*. College Station: Center for Ecological Archaeology, Texas A&M, 2001.

32. W.W. Newcomb, Jr., *The Indians of Texas: From Prehistoric to Modern Times*. Austin: University of Texas Press, 1961, pp. 29-47.

33. http://www.texasbeyondhistory.net/cabez-cooking/index html.

34. "Coahuiltecan Indians." www.tashaonline.org/ handbook/online/articles/bmcah; also Martin Salinas, *Indigenous people of the Rio Grande Delta*. Austin: University of Texas Press, 1990, p. 116.

35. W.W. Newcomb, *The Indians of Texas: From Prehistoric to Modern Times*. Austin: University of Texas Press, 1961, pp. 46, 54-55.

36. Bill Lockhart. "Protohistoric Confusion: A cultural Comparison of the Manso, Suma, and Jumano Indians of the Paso del Norte Region."*Journal of the Southwest*. Vol 39, No. 1 [Spring 1997], p.123.

37. Herbert Eugene Bolton. *Spanish Explorations in the Southwest, 1542-1706.* New York: Charles Scribner's Sons, 1916, p. 175."Foraging Peoples: Chisos and Mansos." *Texas Beyond History.*

38. "Foraging Peoples: Chisos and Mansos." *Texas Beyond History.*

39. Jay W. Sharp, "Life on the Margin Part II", Desert USA website. https://www.desertusa.com/ind1/ ind_new/ind16.html.

40. Mineral resources of the Organ Mountains Wilderness Study Area, Dona Ana County, New Mexico, U.S. Geological Survey Bulletin 1735.

41. New Mexico Mines website.

42. Sierra County Recreation and Tourism website, "Hot Springs in Truth or Consequences".

43. David I. Portillo and Dr. Donald Pepion, "Origins of the Piros and Ethno-History", paper presented at UC Berkeley Symposium 2004.

44. Portillo and Pepion, page 9, quoting C.L. Riley, *Rio del Norte; People of the Upper Rio Grande from Earliest Times to the Pueblo Revolt* (1999).

45. Portillo and Pepion, page 10.

46. Michael P. Marshal & Henry J. Walt, *Rio Abajo: Prehistory and History of a Rio Grande Province* (Santa Fe: New Mexico Historical Preservation Program, 1984), p 248.

47. History of Embroidery website, "Pre-contact Embroidery" https://sarweb.org/embroidery/history/precontactem broidery/designs.htm.

48. "Ancient Art by TM1ssKDMac", 2015 hikearizona.com.

49. D. Clark Wernecke, *"Pleistocene figurative art in the Americas: some cautions"*, Rock Art Research 2015 – Volume 32, Number 1, p. 22.

50. Elia W. Peattie, *The Story of America*, Chicago: R.S. King Publishing Company, 1889, p.235.

51. Connie A. Woodhouse, et al., Proceedings of the National Academy of Sciences, vol. 107, no. 50, December 14, 2010, "A 1,200-year perspective of 21st century drought in southwestern North America"

52. Marc Simmons, "Trail Dust: Mural art of the prehistoric pueblos" The New Mexican, Posted online: Friday, February 22, 2008.

53. Adobe Gallery website, referring to Barton Wright, *Kachinas: A Hopi Artist's Documentary,* [page 160].

54. Wikipedia "Chakwaina", citing Seymore H Koenig, (2005). *Acculturation in the Navajo Eden: New Mexico, 1550-1750*. New York: YBK Publishers; and McDonald, Dedra S. (1998). "Intimacy and Empire: Indian-African Interaction in Spanish Colonial New Mexico, 1500-1800". *American Indian Quarterly* 22 (1/2): 134–156.

55. David H. Brown, Santería Enthroned: Art, Ritual and Innovation in an Afro-Cuban Religion, p. 189.

56. http://navajopeople.org/blog/navajo-creation-story-the-first-world-nihodilhil-black-world/

57. http://navajobusiness.com/pdf/FstFctspdf/A%20Brief%20History.pdf.

58. Gilberto Benito Cordova, "Those Who Have Gone: Indians of Abiquiu", Southwest Crossroads website.

59. J. A. Jeancon, (1923), Excavations in the Chama Valley, New Mexico: Smithsonian Inst.. Bur. Am. Ethnology Bull. 81, pp. 34, 75-76.

60. "Tierra Amarilla - Southwest Crossroads Spotlight", Southwest Crossroads website.

61. http://navajobusiness.com/pdf/FstFctspdf/A%20Brief%20History.pdf.

62. New Mexico Geological Society – Eleventh Field Conference, Carle H. Dane, "Early Explorations of Rio Arriba County, New Mexico and Adjacent Parts of Southern Colorado", pp.117-118.

63. David Imhotep, Ph.D., Forward by Dr. Clyde Winters, *The First Americans were Africans: Documented Evidence*, Author House, Bloomington Indiana: 2012, p. xix.

64. Paul F. Reed, "Salmon Ruins From Cynthia Irwin-Williams's Vision to a Central Place in the Totah", *Archaeology Southwest*, Vol. 16, Number 2, Spring 2002, page 8.

65. February 25, 2015; 9:55 P.M. email to Ronald Stewart by Donal B. Buchanan, Secy/Treasurer, The Epigraphic Society, and Editor of ESOP; entitled "The Flora Vista Tablets" by Harold S. Gladwin, Epigraphic Society Occasional Papers (ESOP), Vol. 14, pp. 14-21.

66. Cryptozoology Research Team website, an article titled "Messages on Stone—Mammoths and Dinosaurs" by Dennis L. Swift.

67. "The "Elephant Slabs" of New Mexico" by Jason Colavito Blog 9/13/2012.

68. Dr. Barry Fell, "Decipherment of the Flora Vista Tablets", ESOP, Vol. 14, pp. 22-27.

69. David Imhotep, Ph.D., Forward by Dr. Clyde Winters, *The First Americans were Africans: Documented Evidence*, Author House, Bloomington Indiana: 2012, p. xix.

70. Clyde Winters, Ancient Origins: Reconstructing the Story of Humanity's Past, website, "The Elephant Slabs of Flora Vista: Enigmatic Artifacts with Ancient African Origins", 24 July, 2016.

71. Ivan Van Sertima, ed., *Blacks in Science: Ancient and Modern* (*Journal of African Civilizations, Jan. 1, 1983*), Clyde-Ahmad Winters, "The Ancient Manding Script", p. 208.

72. K. Hau, "Pre-Islamic writing in West Africa", Bulletin de l'Institut Fondamental Afrique Noire, t35, ser. B, no. 1, 1973.

73. Tukuler, EgyptSearch.com.

74. Ivan Van Sertima, ed., *Blacks in Science: Ancient and Modern* (*Journal of African Civilizations, Jan. 1, 1983*), Clyde-Ahmad Winters, "The Ancient Manding Script", p. 212.

75. Clyde-Ahmad Winters, "The Ancient Manding Script", *Blacks in Science: Ancient and Modern*, pp. 209-214; and 'Alik Shahadah + Others "Bangam Syllabary", *Scripts of Africa* website.

76. E. B. "Ted" Sayles with Joan Ashby Henley, *Fantasies of Gold: Legends of Treasures and How They Grew*, Tucson: The University of Arizona Press, 1968, p. 92.

77. Bureau of Land Management, Bisti/De-Na-Zin Wilderness Area.

78. http://www.americansouthwest.net/new_mexico/ah-shi-sle-pah/.

79. "Records of the Past", Oct. 1903, Vol. 2, part 10, p. 288.

80. Ekkehart Malotki and Henry D. Wallace, "Columbian Mammoth Petroglyphs From The San Juan River Near Bluff, Utah, United States" *Utah Rock Art*, Volume XXXI, 2012, page 13; and *Rock Art Research* 28(2):143-152 · November 2011.

81. Ekkehart Malotki and Peter D. McIntosh, "Paleoamericans, Pleistocene terraces and Petroglyphs: the case for Ice Age mammoth depictions at Upper Sand Island, Utah, USA",

http://www.fpa.tas.gov.au/__data/assets/pdf_file/00 09/115002/Malotki_and_McIntosh_2015_Paleoame ricans_Pleistocene_Terraces_and_Petroglyphs.pdf.

82. A Hopi Prophecy, http://www.ausbcomp.com/ RedMan/hopi_prophecy.htm.

83. Joseph P. Sanchez, Ph. D., Director of the Spanish Colonial Research Center, University of New Mexico; translated from Fray Francisco Garcés, *Diario, de exploraciones en Arizona y California en los años de 1775 y 1776,* Instituto de Investigaciones Históricas, Mexico, Cuadernos, serie documental / número 6, 1968; or see: *Diario de las ultimas peregrinaciones del Padre Fr. Francisco Garcés, hasta la provincia del Moqui, y noticias de varias nuevas naciones exparcidas hasta el Rio Colorado en California, 1777;* or see a translation by Elliott Coues titled *On the Trail of a Spanish Pioneer: The Diary and Itinerary of Francisco Garces (Missionary Priest) in His Travels Through Sonora, Arizona and California 1775-1776,* vol. 2, p.384.

84. crystalinks.com/hopi.

85. Clyde Ahmed Winters, "*Islam in Early North and South America*", Al-Ittihad, July-October 1977, page 63.

86. Joaquín García Icazbalceta, *Nueva colección,* I, 194-195.

87. Henry R. Wagner, "Fr. Marcos de Niza", New Mexico Historical Review, 2, pp. 222-3.

88. Gregory McNamee, *Grand Canyon Place Names,* Boulder, CO: Johnson Books, 1997, p. 39.

89. *American Anthropologist*, "Anthropological Analysis of Exploration Texts: Cultural Discourse and the Ethnological Import of Fray Marcos de Niza's Journey to Cibola", vol.93, 1991, pp. 636-655.

90. Samuel Hubbard, (1925), *Discoveries Relating to Prehistoric Man by the Doheny Scientific Expedition in the Hava Supai Canyon* (San Francisco, CA: Sunset Press). pp. 12-13; Samuel Hubbard (1926), "African Lions Roamed in Hollywood," *The Dearborn Independent*, 26[35]:12-13,22, June 19.

91. Wikipedia, "Havasupai".

92. Frederick Webb Hodge (1968). *Handbook of American Indians North of Mexico. Scholarly Press. part 2, p. 994.*

93. Timothy Braatz (2003). *Surviving Conquest.* University of Nebraska Press, p. 36.

94. Laura Redish and Orrin Lewis, Native Languages of the Americas, Mojave Indian Fact Sheet website.

95. "Yuman", New World Encyclopedia.

96. William Marder, *Indians in the Americas: The Untold Story*, pp. 14-15.

97. www.economist.con/node/5381851.

98. Paul Barton, "Black Civilizations of Ancient America (Muu-lan), Mexico (Xi)", Race and History website.

99. Black Indians United website, "Malcolm J. Rogers Confirmed Historic Presence of Australo/African Indians Announced Discovery of Black Aborigines Indigenous to North America", from Rogers, 1958

San Diego Union Article, "Who Are The First San Diegans?"

100. Paul Barton, "Descendants of Ancient Africans in Recent America", Race and History website.

101. "The Mythical Menehune of Kaua`I" http://www.donch.com/lulhmenemyth. htm.

102. Luoumala, Menehune of Polynesia, B.P. Museum Bulletin 203. Honolulu 1951: 12; quoted in Handy, Handy, and Pukau 1972: 405.

103. Thomas G. Thrum, *Hawaiian Folk Tales*, 1907, p. 117. http://www.sacred-texts.com/pac/hft/hft13.htm

104. Rich Figel, "Menehune Village Discovery", http://careerchangers. staradvertiserblogs.com/2013/04/01/menehune-village-discovery/.

105. Pedro Alonso Niño, Columbus's pilot, was born in Palos de Moguer, Spain, to a Spanish father and an African slave mother. He explored the coasts of Africa in his early years and he piloted one of Columbus' ships in the expedition of 1492.

106. Words of the Mali *griot* Mamadou Kouyaté, quoted in D. T. Niane, *Sundiata: An Epic of Old Mali A.D. 1217-1237,* from Ivan Van Sertima, *They Came Before Columbus,* page 39.

107. http://carriacou.biz/arawaks-amerindians/

108. Bertha P. Dutton, *Sun Father's Way, The Kiva Murals of Kuaua,* Albuquerque: University of New Mexico Press.

Made in the USA
Middletown, DE
08 January 2019